PIONEER REMINISCENCES

OF

PUGET SOUND

AN ACCOUNT OF THE COMING OF THE FIRST AMERICANS AND THE
ESTABLISHMENT OF THEIR INSTITUTIONS; THEIR ENCOUNT-
ERS WITH THE NATIVE RACE; THE FIRST TREATIES
WITH THE INDIANS AND THE WAR THAT FOLLOW-
ED; SEVEN YEARS OF THE LIFE OF ISAAC I.
STEVENS IN WASHINGTON TERRITORY;
CRUISE OF THE AUTHOR ON PUGET
SOUND FIFTY YEARS AGO;
NISQUALLY HOUSE AND
THE HUDSON BAY
COMPANY.

FROM PERSONAL OBSERVATION DURING FIFTY YEARS RESIDENCE,
CONTEMPORARY PIONEER REMINISCENCES AND
OTHER AUTHENTIC SOURCES.

By EZRA MEEKER

SEATTLE, WASH.

1905

LOWMAN & HANFORD
STATIONERY AND PRINTING CO.
SEATTLE, WASH.

ISBN 0-939806-01-0

DEDICATION

To the intrepid pioneer men and women of the Northwest,
this work is respectfully dedicated.

Seattle, Washington, 1905.

EZRA MEEKER

Introduction to 1980 Edition

Ezra Meeker was an Oregon Trail pioneer, and it affected his life forever after.

Born in 1830 in Ohio, Meeker grew up in Indiana and married Eliza Jane Sumner there when he was only 21. With the lure of free land leading them on, they came to Oregon Territory in 1852, along with a month-old son, Marion.

The five-month trip along the Oregon Trail was a journey of high adventure for Meeker. He later said he left Indiana a boy and arrived in Oregon a man. The strength he gained and the self-reliance he developed at that time helped him later when adversity struck.

Meeker first settled his family in a cabin at Kalama, and later on McNeil Island. Still later, he took a donation land claim in what is now the Fern Hill area of Tacoma, but it was poor, badly-drained land and when the Indian Wars of 1855-56 broke out, Meeker was glad to take his family to the safety of Steilacoom.

There he went into the mercantile business with his father, Jacob, and his brother, Oliver. After the war, they decided to continue in the business, and borrowing money, they sent Oliver to San Francisco for supplies. On the return trip, the steamer ran into a storm and sank, Oliver drowned and the supplies were lost — and so was the Meekers' business.

In 1862, Ezra Meeker brought his little family into the Puyallup Valley where he had purchased a squatter's cabin. They were so poor that Meeker had no overcoat, but wore an old blanket with a hole cut in the center to fit over his head.

His poverty did not last. In 1865 he planted a handful of hop roots from a sack consigned to his father, and started on a career that led to his being known as "The Hop King of the World."

At one time, he had more land planted to hops than any other man in Washington. He became a hop broker, wrote a book on hop culture and made four trips to England in connection with the hop business. On one of the trips, he and Eliza Jane were presented to Queen Victoria. One year, he made more than $500,000 from his hop business.

He built a stately home of 17 rooms in Puyallup that became the social center of the Northwest. The home is in a remarkable state of preservation and is being restored and maintained by the Ezra Meeker Historical Society. It is on the National Register of Historic Sites.

In the early 1890s, an infestation of hop aphids and problems with mildew brought an end to the lucrative hop industry of western Washington. Although he lost most of his money in the hop crop failure and the economic depression of the time, Meeker was not daunted.

He joined the rush to the Klondike gold fields in 1897, but not as a miner. He and Eliza Jane dried vegetables and packed them in cans to take to the Yukon where he sold food to the hungry miners. He gained a small fortune in this enterprise but lost it when he succumbed to the lure of gold and sank it into a mining claim that did not pay off.

Meeker had written a pamphlet about western Washington that was instrumental in bringing the railroad to the northwest and, when he returned from the Klondike, he started writing a history of this area as he had known it. *Pioneer Reminiscences of Puget Sound* and *The Tragedy of Leschi* were published in one volume in 1905 when he was 74 years of age.

Meeker had a vivid memory of the early pioneer days in Washington Territory. He had served on the jury that first tried Leschi and was one of two jurors who voted for his acquittal. His friendship with the Indians and his concepts of religion and the rights of minorities marked him as a man of few prejudices.

A self-taught man (he had only a few months formal schooling) he wrote interestingly about pioneer life, which he had enjoyed even though it was extremely laborious. He became a prolific writer, even wrote and published a novel when he was 95 years old. *Pioneer Reminiscences* is, undoubtedly, his best work.

In 1906, when he was 75 years old, he drove an ox team back over the Oregon Trail, making speeches and establishing markers of the trail, preserving it for future generations.

He made a number of other trips across the country by the several means of transportation, including one by airplane in 1924 when he was 93 years old. He frequently generated national headlines, once when he drove his ox team and wagon to the White House where he met President Theodore Roosevelt.

He was in the process of making a deal with Henry Ford to drive one of Ford's experimental cars across the country when he became ill in 1928 and came home to Seattle where he died, just two years and a month before he could attain his final ambition, to live to be 100 years of age.

He traveled his last trail to Woodbine Cemetery in Puyallup where he lies beside Eliza Jane, under a headstone that bears the inscription: "They came this way to win and hold the West."

— LORI PRICE,
President, Ezra Meeker Historical Society, Puyallup, WA.

ILLUSTRATIONS

FRONTISPIECE.

TABLE OF CONTENTS

CHAPTER IV.

CRUISE ON PUGET SOUND.

CHAPTER V.

CRUISE ON PUGET SOUND.—*Continued.*

CHAPTER VI.

CRUISE ON PUGET SOUND.—*Continued.*

CHAPTER VII.

CRUISE ON PUGET SOUND.—*Continued.*

CHAPTER VIII.

CRUISE ON PUGET SOUND.—*Continued.*

CHAPTER IX.

FROM COLUMBIA RIVER.

CHAPTER X.

THE SECOND CABIN.

CHAPTER XI.

TRIP THROUGH THE NATCHESS PASS.

CHAPTER XII.

TRIP THROUGH THE NATCHESS PASS—*Continued.*

CONTENTS.

CHAPTER XVII.

FIRST IMMIGRANTS THROUGH THE NATCHESS PASS, 1853.

CHAPTER XVIII.

BUILDING OF THE NATCHESS PASS ROAD.

CHAPTER XIX.

BUILDING OF THE NATCHESS PASS ROAD.—*Concluded.*

CHAPTER XX.

THE MUD WAGON ROAD.

CHAPTER XXI.

THE FRASER RIVER STAMPEDE.

CHAPTER XXII.

THE OLD SETTLERS' MEETING.

CHAPTER XXIII.

A CHAPTER ON NAMES.

CHAPTER XXIV.

PIONEER RELIGIOUS EXPERIENCES AND INCIDENTS.

CHAPTER XXV.

WILD ANIMALS.

CONTENTS.

CHAPTER XXVI.

THE MORNING SCHOOL.

Chapter for Boys and Girls—Peter Smith's Visit—Why! We
Have School Now—Father Teaches Us—The Old School
Master—The Early Rising—The Happy Youngsters—The
Old Log School House—Work Before School—The Christ-
mas Trees—The Fourth of July Celebrations—The Home-
Made Shoes—The Home-Made Pegs—The Home Music
—Song Fifty Years Ago. 194

INTRODUCTORY

THE HISTORY OF A HISTORY.

Four years ago to-day I arrived at the ripe age of three score years and ten, supposed to be the limit of life. Finding that I possessed more ambition than strength, and that my disposition for a strenuous life was greater than my power of physical endurance, I naturally turned to other fields of work, that condition of life so necessary for the welfare and happiness of the human race.

Many years before it had been my ambition to write our earlier experiences of pioneer life on Puget Sound, and not necessarily for the printer, but because I wanted to, but never could find time; and so when the change came and my usual occupation was gone, what else would I be more likely to do than to turn to my long delayed work, the more particularly being admonished that it must be done soon or not at all. And so, in a cheerful, happy mood, I entered again into the domain of pioneer life, and began writing. But this is not history, you will say. True, but we will come to that by and by.

I had, during the summer of 1853, with an inexperienced companion, in an open boat—a frail skiff built with our own hands—crossed the path of Theodore Winthrop, spending more than a month on a cruise from Olympia to the Straits and return, while that adventurous traveler and delightful writer had with a crew of Indians made the trip from Port Townsend to Fort Nisqually in a canoe. I had followed Winthrop a year later through the Natchess Pass to the Columbia River and beyond, alone, except a companion pony that carried my sack of hard bread for food, the saddle blanket for my bed and myself across the turbulent rivers, and on easy grades. If Winthrop could write such a beautiful book, "The Canoe and the Saddle," based upon such a trip, with Indians to paddle his canoe on the Sound, and with an attendant and three horses through the mountains, why should not my own experience of such a trip be interesting to my own children and their children's children? And so I wrote these trips.

Did you ever, when hungry, taste of a dish of fruit, a luscious, ripe, highly flavored apple for instance, that seemed only to whet but not satisfy your appetite? I know you have, and so can appreciate my feelings when these stories were written. I craved more of pioneer life experience, and so I went back to the earlier scenes, a little earlier only—to the trip in a flat boat down the Columbia River from The Dalles to the first cabin, where Kalama town now stands; to the pack on our backs from the Columbia to the Sound; to the three times passing the road to and fro to get the wife and baby to tidewater—what a charm that word tidewater had for me with a vision of the greatness of opportunities of the seaboard—and I may say it has never lost its charm—of the great world opened up before me, and so we were soon again housed in the little cabin with its puncheon floor, "cat-and-clay" chimney, and clapboard roof; its surroundings of scenery; of magnificent forests and of constantly moving life, the Indians with their happy song and fishing parties.

All this and more, too, I wrote, every now and then getting over to the Indian question. How could I help it? We had been treated civilly, and I may say, kindly, by them from the very outset, when we, almost alone, were their white neighbors. I had been treated generously by some, and had always found them ready to reciprocate in acts of kindness, and so we had come to respect our untutored neighbors and to sympathize with them in their troubles. Deep troubles came to them when the treaty-making period arrived, and a little later upon all of us, when war came, to break up all our plans and amicable relations. As I began to write more about the Indians and their ways, a step further brought me to the consideration of our Territorial government and the government officials and their acts. It gradually dawned upon me this was a more important work than writing of humble individuals; that the history of our commonwealth was by far a more interesting theme, and more profitable to the generations to follow than recording of private achievements of the pioneer. It was but a step further until I realized that I was fairly launched upon the domain of history, and that I must need be more painstaking and more certain of my facts, and so then came a long rest for my pen and a long search of the records, of old musty letters, of no less old musty books, of forgetful minds of the pioneers left, and again I was carried away into the almost forgotten past.

An authoress once told me that she never named her book until after it was written. I could not then understand why, but I now do. While writing of pioneer life I could think of no other title than something like this: "Pioneer Life on Puget Sound Fifty Years Ago," a pretty long title, but that was what the writing treated of. But when I got on the Indian question and came to realize what a splendid true story was wrapped up in the darkness of impending oblivion; how the Indians had been wronged; how they had fought for their homes and won them; how the chief actors had been sacrificed, but the tribes had profited—I again became enthusiastic over my theme and over my ready-made heroes, and before I realized it, lo! a new name took possession of my mind and rang in it until there was born the title, "The Tragedy of Leschi."

When I come to think of it, that here were tribes that had never shed white men's blood until grim war came, and that then they refused to make war on their old neighbors, and that but one non-combatant settler had

lost his life after the first day of frenzy of the Muckleshoot band at the massacre of White River, that here
were men we called savages, fighting for a cause, but
threw themselves on the track of the military arm of
the government and not against helpless settlers.   I
had myself been in their power and remained unharmed.
I knew other of my neighbors also that had been exposed
and remained unmolested; surely to tell the truth about
such people is no more than justice and I said to myself,
I will write it down and prove what I write by the
records and the best obtainable witnesses alive, and
having done so, will print it, two books in one, two
titles, yet but one volume, "Pioneer Reminiscences of
Puget Sound; The Tragedy of Leschi."

It is natural that in the stirring times of early
days opinions would differ; that neighbors, and even
members of families would look upon events from dif-
fering points of view, and so out of this maze I have
tried to state exact facts and draw just conclusions.
The chapter of this history begins with the creation of
the Territory and ends with Governor Stevens' official
life in the Territory in the period concerned.   During
that period, treaties were made with the Indians, the
war with them was fought; massacres horrid to con-
template were perpetrated by the Indians and whites—
by the Indians at the outbreak, and the whites later—
murders were committed; martial law proclaimed, our
courts invaded with armed men, judges dragged from
the bench; our governor in turn brought before the
courts, fined and reprieved by himself, and many other
happenings unique in history are related, and so, when
my labor was finished and my pen laid aside, my only
regret was that the work had not been undertaken earlier
in life when memory served more accurately, and my
contemporaries were more numerous.

                                    E. MEEKER.
Seattle, Dec. 29th, 1904.

MY SECOND FORE-WORD

"Why did you go to Puget Sound in that early day?" I have been asked a thousand times, I verily believe; so often, at least, that I feel prompted to write about it, although no very plausible reason may appear.

It is an American instinct to want to better one's condition; we may say that it is a worldwide instinct that pervades the human breast, but more particularly that of an American. The words or phrase, to "better his condition," may mean many things. It may mean he seeks a better climate; or seeks a better soil; or for better health; or a future better market. In a word, in so many ways that we become lost in the attempt to enumerate them.

"But " says one, "you had the whole of the Middle West to choose from fifty years ago, and why you should run over such a vast field and take such chances is an enigma to me." And so it is to many who participated in the great movement across the plains to this day.

The answer is not hard to find if one but seeks the moving motives that govern mankind. It is true that no such movement can be found in history where so great a number moved so great a distance as was witnessed in the immigration to the Pacific Coast in '52; and so we must need to look for exceptional causes governing this exceptional movement.

It was like an army moving out to battle and burning their bridges behind them. When the Missouri River was crossed, or at least when a short distance out, a

return became impossible; the road was choked by
teams all moving one way, or if not, left small parties
returning at the mercy of the Indians, to be robbed, possibly murdered.

The motive prompting the movement had been gathering force for years. The great contrast in the early
days, before cheap transportation came, between conditions on the Atlantic seaboard and the interior, set
men to thinking about the great unoccupied territory
within the reach of the Pacific—within reach of the
world's market, within reach of the ocean's highway—
and fired the imagination of the would-be immigrant.
Here was the opportunity of a lifetime to get to the
front and pick the choicest fruits of the earth. I say,
and yet think, they were right, although many missed
the mark. Another potent cause was the climate that
was pictured in such glowing terms in contrast with
the conditions existing in the Middle West. Then there
came the incentive to better one's condition financially;
get land; get gold; get choice locations. The argu-
ment was, there must be such opportunities in so large
a country so sparsely settled.

Then another class, that had to take every third day
off to shake with the ague, while the process was going
on of turning the virgin soil of the Middle West, formed
no inconsiderable number that counted this the moving
cause that governed their actions—a search for health.
Coupled with all this was the American desire for adventure, planted in the breasts of so many of the pioneers of the frontier, that some were willing to undertake the trip just for the fun of the thing; but they did
not find it very funny before they got through. But let
us now consider the start and what happened.

"Do you think it safe to prepare for the trip?" This
question was asked in a rather hesitating manner, as
though the speaker felt it was hardly proper at the time
to make such an inquiry of the person addressed.

"Why, yes; I think so. Baby will be three weeks old to-morrow, and it will take three weeks to get ready. I think it will be all right, don't you?"

"Just like a woman," I said, "to answer one question by asking another; but I think that settles it, and we will go to Oregon this year."

This little talk took place in a small cabin near the Des Moines River, in Iowa, with a good deal more of like kind, between the little wife and young husband, the writer of this story, during the first week of April, 1852, and upon the conclusion to be reached depended whether we should become pioneers and go to Oregon or remain in the harsh Iowa climate and make our home on the prairies of the Middle West.

It is not the intention to write an autobiography of my life, though personal experiences will be drawn upon that are intimately interwoven with events in the further West for the fifty years following the incident just related. I could not do otherwise if I would, and write of the conditions of the pioneer life that followed.

So the preparations began in earnest for the great trip across the plains. Buck bought the outfit and I the team.

When as a boy I used to delight in breaking the calves to play work, and later the larger steers to sure work, little did I think the experience then gained would in after life stand me so well in hand to save me from danger and discomfort.

A few days sufficed to purchase four unbroken steers and four unbroken cows, and get the yokes fitted, with everything ready for the start during the last week of April, 1852.

"What are you going to do now?" asked Buck, as we halted for the first night's camp.

"Unyoke the cattle, of course, and turn them out to graze," I answered, and at the same time began preparing to do so.

"But you will never get them in the yoke again if you turn them loose here!" my friend excitedly replied.

While I contended it would not do to leave them in the yoke, Buck as firmly insisted that we must not turn them loose. At this juncture a stranger, camped near by, interrupted, and said he and his men would help us to yoke up in the morning; that his animals were gentle and that we would have no difficulty, and so the cattle were turned out on the range and we gave attention to the making of our first camp.

This stranger, the peacemaker, we soon came to know as one that would do to tie to, and for the next two months, and for a thousand miles, we traveled and camped near together, and thereafter never a word of contention passed between the three. Thomas McAuley —for that was his name—had, like William Buck and myself, fitted out light and with unbroken cattle, which proved to be a great boon to both of us, as we moved out on the long journey.

The trip across the plains has been so often written that it would seem the whole ground has been covered, though from start to finish it was pioneer life in dead earnest. Nevertheless, the after-experience would seem incomplete without some mention of how we got to the pioneer field of the farther West, and a little of the experience on the way.

"It will be necessary for your own safety to take yourself away from here, and that quite quick."

The individual addressed, who was no less a person than the sheriff of an Iowa county bordering on the Missouri River near Council Bluffs, concluded that discretion was the better part of valor, and at once obeyed the mandate of an orderly mob who had dug out of the sands an abandoned scow in which to cross the river, which an alleged owner concluded to take charge of as soon as in good running order. The crossing of the Missouri was the first real danger encountered. After waiting a week to get across with the ferry, and after seeing several lives sacrificed, our little crowd concluded to help themselves, with the result mentioned while preparing for a first trip.

The two sisters, Eliza and Margaret McAuley, with the little wife and baby, were set across the river on the first load and left to watch the outfit to prevent it falling into the hands of the pilfering Pawnee Indians. Then and there came near being the baptism of blood, figuratively, which they said seemed the only way to drive the thieves off. The show of guns in a most threatening attitude of the three women had the desired effect, though the guns were not loaded, and they were left unmolested.

It took every hand to man the boat, but we crossed without loss of life or property.

The number that crossed that river into the Indian country will never be known. We ascertained by the scribbling on rocks and other signs left that the army was nearly or quite five hundred miles long, and, no inconsiderable part of the way, three columns deep. The crowd was so great that at times all the wagons could not get into one track, especially during the morning hour, and so it often came about that there were parallel columns moving, usually in close proximity, with resultant strife for possession of the main beaten track. Moving columns of loose stock on either side of the road, of which there were driven great numbers at the start, added much to the discomfort and strife among the people.

I say at the start, because it was not long before the loss of stock was fearful to relate, and thinned their number, as likewise the teams, and caused many hundreds of wagons to be left standing by the roadside. With this loss of teams soon came the abandonment of all sorts of superfluous property, so that the road became lined with piles of all sorts of household goods, and later provisions, in large quantities.

The greater body of the immigrants formed themselves into large companies and elected captains. These combinations soon began to dissolve and reform, to dissolve again, until it seemed as though everybody was for himself, and I had liked to have said, "the devil for them all."

When, to add to the contentions going on, there came the epidemic of cholera, it appeared as though the people lost their reason and all sense of the responsibility resting upon them, like a panic-stricken army (as they were) fleeing from dangers they knew not how nor where —only to get away from where they were.

The result was a continued strife for mastery of the road, to see who could get ahead and who could travel farthest in a day, to try "to get out of this cholera."

But I must not tarry to tell too much about this, else we will never get across the plains with this story.

Suffice it to say that the loss of life and property was fearful to relate. In one camping place we counted fifty-odd fresh graves, none of which bore date of more than the previous week; and as for the carcasses of dead stock, certainly such could be counted by the thousands, for one might almost say literally we were never out of the sight or smell of them for a thousand miles on the trip.

Buck and McAuley were both older than myself, though both of them bachelors. They were cool, brave men. One of the sisters bordered on the old-maidish list, but never did a more courageous woman live, as after emergencies showed, though coupled with true ladylike character and modest demeanor.

The married man and the little wife were the youngest of the party (except the baby), and in all conscience were young enough indeed to assume such a responsibility; but we were there on the plains, the step had been taken and could not be retraced, and so with sobering surrounding circumstances and with the close circle of associates of great worth, disaster did not overtake us. And I will now say, in dismissing this part of the subject, that we did not throw away a pound of provisions or property of any kind, nor lose a hoof of stock.

There came a little touch of romance connected with the separation of Buck and myself at the big bend of Bear River. Buck was 28 years old, and according to commonly accepted belief a confirmed bachelor. He was in some respects an eccentric man, and as intense in his dislikes as he was in his friendships—so scrupulously neat and orderly that some of the thoughtless were ready to dub him as "old maidish," or bordering on the dude. Those who knew him well knew that there did not exist the least particle of either of these characteristics in his conduct.

One of the sisters met at our first camp and with whom we afterwards traveled so far, I could see attracted the attention of Buck in spite of himself, but the usual observer could not detect by his actions the least sign; but somehow or other the little wife and I came to feel we knew that Buck had lost his heart. He was passionately fond of children, and so uproriously so of our baby that casual neighbor campers would naturally think he was the father and husband, and not for a moment of the boyish-looking person in the company. Buck became the camp-man, one might say by natural selection. He was so handy, cleanly, untiring, never lagging until the last chore was done, the last tent secure, water provided, fuel secured for the morrow if to be had; in a word, he was not the man to leave anything undone that could be done for the convenience of the company—the McAuleys and ourselves.

At the very start he insisted that he wanted to go to California, but said he did not want to "keep bach" on the plains, and upon short acquaintance had agreed that he would go to Oregon with us (wife and me and baby) for the sake of company, and thence to California alone.

But as we approached the forks of the road the little wife nudged the young husband to whisper: "Don't you think we might let Buck go to California with the McAuleys?"

"Why do you ask that question; he hasn't said anything about it, has he?" asked the young husband.

"Oh, no, nor neither will he; but I know."

"Know what?"

"Well, I know he is—"

"Is what?" But the question remained unanswered, for the little wife knew that the young husband knew as well as she did what was "what."

Buck blushed scarlet to the very ears when I told him that we knew he would like to take the left-hand road that was then near ahead of us, and go to California with the McAuleys. And that was the only sign he gave, except, as one might say, an indescribable expression of the eyes for the moment, which, however, soon disappeared.

At the last camp we tarried together for many days, just turned loose for a big visit; but there were scarcely any dry eyes in the camp when good-byes were said to the baby as Buck and McAuley drove out on the California road.

We kept up our acquaintance until his death, which occurred a good many years ago. The last time I saw him was at his splendid home near San Filipe, California, a veritable fairy nook of fruit and flowers, showing the same orderly, artistic hand; but he was then a sure-enough bachelor over sixty years old, and he never married. He inquired about the baby, who was then married and had children of his own, and who is now a grandfather, but nothing was said about the episode of the plains; that is, as to that particular occurrence. Of course, we always lived the trip over again when we met.

Buck is the man that introduced the honey bee into Oregon and Washington, and I think California also. He sent me five swarms by steamer from San Francisco a few years after our trip, two of which I kept and sold the remainder for $125.00 for each swarm. It is a curious fact that before the advent of the American settlers no honey bees were found west of the Rocky Mountains. Some one attempted to bring a swarm by wagon across the plains, but Buck made two trips to the Atlantic seaboard via the Isthmus of Panama, and each trip brought a large number of swarms. He was a man that could accomplish such a feat if anyone in this wide world could. I loved Buck almost to the point of idolatry, and I may say we formed a very small but select mutual admiration society that continued until his death. The last time I saw him away from home was at Puyallup some fifteen years ago. He had been robbed in Tacoma and came up for money to take him home. The humor of the incident was to see him hesitate to ask even this small favor, so independent in spirit was he, but he always took pleasure in bestowing a favor apparently on anyone, be he friend or stranger. He was one of nature's noblemen.

One morning while at breakfast, thirty years or more after the incidents first related, a letter was placed on the table and immediately opened, and read in part as follows:

"Ezra Meeker, my friend of ye Auld Lang Syne, Puyallup, Washington Territory:

"I have just read an item in a paper about an Ezra Meeker of Puyallup, Washington Territory, and have wondered if that is the Ezra Meeker I knew in my girlhood days. I suppose you will have looked at the signature to this letter to ascertain who your correspondent is, and are as yet none the wiser. (I had done that very thing and could not for

the life of me tell who the writer was.) Well, I thought
first to ask you how you are, is your wife living and are
you well, and how have you prospered (still a mystery),
and how is that baby, Dick?"

That let the whole secret out. It was one of the Mc-
Auley girls that was writing, and so the letter was read
aloud from beginning to end to the little wife who sat
opposite at the table.

The letter continued "that she was married and had
five children, two of whom had just graduated," and
much more of deep interest to the recipients of the letter, but not of particular interest to the general reader,
finishing with "an earnest hope we may some time meet
and become acquainted again."

"I will go and see her," the little wife said; and sure
enough, the visit was made, although it involved nearly
fifteen hundred miles of travel.

One of the sisters, the letter told us, was dead long
before, but nothing was said about Buck, or much of the
trip after we had separated at the big bend of Bear
River.

Of the meeting and greeting that followed little need
be said. Pen cannot describe the feelings of pioneers
upon meeting after a long separation, as time passes.
After a short interval of time there is a bond of union
that cannot be described, to be understood by those outside the class to which this peculiar experience belongs.

The incident illustrates how complete the isolation
of the pioneer who goes to a new country without post
roads (or, for that matter, roads of any kind), or post-
offices, or even towns, the names and locations of which
are all strange to the friends left behind and to the outside world of civilization.

Without question there were real hardships to be endured on that trip that were unavoidable. The dust at
times was intolerable, the water often bad, the heat op-
pressive, the road heavy and fatigue great; neverthe-

less, the greater part of these discomforts could be overcome or avoided, and were overcome by great numbers.

Three incidents have been so indelibly fixed in my mind that I feel prompted to first review them before attempting to follow the long train of events that ensued—the night stampede of the buffaloes, the crossing of the Snake River in our wagon beds, and the trip in a flatboat down the Columbia River from The Dalles to the Cascades.

It is difficult to realize that of those vast herds of buffalo we saw, none of their kind are left. Words can give no adequate idea as to number in sight from favorable points of view. As far as the eye could reach the animals would appear like the most tiny little specks in the distance, and finally in a further field show as a shaded tint on the landscape. There seemed to be no end to them. For hundreds of miles at times these herds were in sight, interspersed with the antelope, a lovely, graceful creature to behold, in great contrast to their companions afield, the ugly, ill-shapen buffaloes.

The incident of the stampede alluded to occurred one night several hundred miles out on our journey. On that particular evening the wagons had been placed in a semi-circle, with ropes connecting to make a complete inclosure. The usual guards sent with the stock when kept out on the range were asleep, save one sentinel. The first intimation of danger came when every hoof of stock within the enclosure sprang to their feet as if they had become possessed of an evil spirit. The resultant confusion and the roar of the approaching herd awoke every inmate in or under every wagon or tent to rally in undress to weak points of the enclosure. To hear that sound is never to forget it. Like the roar of the heaviest tornado, one could scarcely tell the direction from which it came, or the distance from which it emanated; neither the direction in which it was moving, and all we could do was to prepare for the onslaught, which might or might not strike us, and await results. Fortunately the great herd passed to one side of us, though very near, so near we thought it was surely upon us, though we escaped entirely unharmed and without the loss of a single animal. Not so with many of our camping neighbors, who lost heavily in stock stampeded, and some of which they never recovered, and detained their trains for days.

Snake River just below Salmon Falls is a comparatively placid stream, though quite too deep for fording, and very wide. We knew if we crossed over we must cross back in a hundred miles or so, and thus encounter a double danger. But the temptation of good feed for a season for our almost famished stock was too strong, and we began the preparation for the crossing. The incident I can most distinctly remember of all is when I reversed the usual order and ran my wagon into the river over the wagon bed and gradually moved out into deep water until the whole was afloat. The bed was so deeply laden that the least ripple in the water would slop over the sides, whilst I rowed the whole over to the opposite side of the river. How it came it did not swamp I can now scarcely realize, but I know only that I got over safely and that very minute wished myself back on the other side, for I knew not what was ahead of me on the crossing further down the river.

We got all our little party over safely, and safely back again, but we all took a long breath, a sigh of relief, when the last wagon bed was landed with the last remnant of the outfit.

Not so fortunate were many of our neighboring fellow travelers, many of whom lost property, and some their lives. Give me a wide berth from crossing Snake River in a wagon bed, is my prayer.

Strange as it may appear, yet it is true, that in the face of all this danger, many were inclined to dispose of their teams and start down that river in their wagon beds—stark crazy, I should say—all of whom soon lost everything, and many their lives. Those who did escape came near starving before they reached the immigrant road. One boy, now a respected citizen of Tacoma, with a part of the family not drowned, was on the range for seven days without food other than roots and herbage, plucked as they traveled. Many never were heard of afterwards.

The third incident alluded to was the voyage down the Columbia River in a flatboat, from The Dalles to the Cascades, and is related in the chapter following, "Floating Down the River."

PIONEER REMINISCENCES

OF

PUGET SOUND

CHAPTER I.

Floating Down the River.

On a September day of 1852 an assemblage of persons could be seen encamped on the banks of the great Columbia, at The Dalles, now a city of no small pretensions, but then only a name for the peculiar configuration of country adjacent to and including the waters of the great river.

One would soon discover this assemblage was constantly changing. Every few hours stragglers came in from off the dusty road, begrimed with the sweat of the brow commingled with particles of dust driven through the air, sometimes by a gentle breeze and then again by a violent gale sweeping up the river through the mountain gap of the Cascade Range. A motley crowd these people were, almost cosmopolitan in nationality, yet all vestige of race peculiarities or race prejudices ground away in the mill of adversity and trials common to all alike in common danger. And yet, the dress and appearance of this assemblage were as varied as the human countenance and as unique as the great mountain scenery before them. Some were clad in scanty attire as soiled with the dust as their brows; others, while with better pretensions, lacked some portions of dress required in civilized life. Here a matronly dame with clean apparel would be without shoes, or there, perhaps, the husband without the hat or perhaps both shoes and hat absent; there the youngsters of all ages, making no pretensions to genteel clothing other than to cover their nakedness. An expert's ingenuity would be taxed to the utmost to discover either the texture or original color of the clothing of either juvenile or adult, so prevailing was the patch work and so inground the particles of dust and sand from off the plains.

Some of these people were buoyant and hopeful in the anticipation of meeting friends whom they knew were awaiting them at their journey's end, while others were downcast and despondent as their thoughts went back to their old homes left behind, and the struggle now so near ended, and forward to the (to them) unknown land ahead. Some had laid friends and relatives tenderly away in the shifting sands, who had fallen by the wayside, with the certain knowledge that with many the spot selected by them would not be the last resting place for the bones of the loved ones. The hunger of the wolf had been appeased by the abundance of food from the fallen cattle that lined the trail for a thousand miles or more, or from the weakened beasts of the immigrants that constantly submitted to capture by the relentless native animals.

The story of the trip across the plains in 1852 is both interesting and pathetic, but I have planned to write of life after the journey rather than much about the journey itself; of the trials that beset the people after their five months' struggle on the tented field of two thousand miles of marching was ended, where, like on the very battlefield, the dead lay in rows of fifties or more; where the trail became so lined with fallen animals, one could scarcely be out of sight or smell of carrion; where the sick had no respite from suffering, nor the well from fatigue. But this oft told story is a subject of itself, treated briefly to the end we may have space to tell what happened when the journey was ended.

The constant gathering on the bank of the Columbia and constant departures of the immigrants did not materially change the numbers encamped, nor the general appearance. The great trip had moulded this army of homeseekers into one homogeneous mass, a common brotherhood, that left a lasting impression upon the participants, and, although few are left now, not one but will greet an old comrade as a brother indeed, and in fact, with hearty and oftentimes tearful congratulations.

We camped but two days on the bank of the river. When I say we, let it be understood that I mean myself, my young wife, and the little baby boy, who was but seven weeks old when the start was made from near Eddyville, Iowa. Both were sick, the mother from gradual exhaustion during the trip incident to motherhood, and the little one in sympathy, doubtless drawn from the mother's breast.

Did you ever think of the wonderful mystery of the inner action of the mind, how some impressions once made seem to remain, while others gradually fade away, like the twilight of a summer sunset, until finally lost? And then how seemingly trivial incidents will be fastened upon one's memory while others of more importance we would recall if we could, but which have faded forever from our grasp? I can well believe all readers have had this experience, and so will be prepared to receive with leniency the confession of an elderly gentleman, (I will not say old), when he says that most of the incidents are forgotten and few remembered. I do not remember the embarking on the great scow for the float down the river to the Cascades, but vividly remember, as though it were but yes-

terday, incidents of the voyage. We all felt (I now
mean the immigrants who took passage) that now our
journey was ended. The cattle had been unyoked for the
last time. The wagons had been rolled to the last
bivouac; the embers of the last camp fire had died out;
the last word of gossip had been spoken, and now, we
were entering a new field with new present experience,
and with new expectancy for the morrow.

The scow or lighter upon which we took passage was
decked over, but without railing, a simple, smooth surface upon which to pile our belongings, which, in
the great majority of cases made but a very small
showing. I think there must have been a dozen
families, or more, of sixty or more persons, principally women and children, as the young men (and
some old ones, too) were struggling on the mountain
trail to get the teams through to the west side. The
whole deck surface of the scow was covered with the
remnants of the immigrants' outfits, which in turn were
covered by the owners, either sitting or reclining upon
their possessions, leaving but scant room to change posi-
tion or move about in any way.

Did you ever, reader, have the experience when some
sorrow overtook you, or when some disappointment had
been experienced, or when deferred hopes had not been
realized, or sometimes even without these and from
some unknown, subtle cause, feel that depression of
spirits that for lack of a better name we call "the blues?"
When the world ahead looked dark; when hope seemed
extinguished and the future looked like a blank? Why
do I ask this question? I know you all to a greater or
less degree have had just this experience. Can you
wonder that after our craft had been turned loose upon
the waters of the great river, and begun floating lazily
down with the current, that such a feeling as that
described would seize us as with an iron grip? We
were like an army that had burned the bridges behind

them as they marched, and with scant knowledge of what lay in the track before them. Here we were, more than two thousand miles from home, separated by a trackless, uninhabited waste of country, impossible for us to retrace our steps. Go ahead we must, no matter what we were to encounter. Then, too, the system had been strung up for months, to duties that could not be avoided or delayed, until many were on the verge of collapse. Some were sick and all reduced in flesh from the urgent call for camp duty, and lack of variety of food. Such were the feelings of the motley crowd of sixty persons as we slowly neared that wonderful crevice through which the great river flows while passing the Cascade mountain range.

For myself, I can truly say, that the trip had not drawn on my vitality as I saw with so many. True, I had been worked down in flesh, having lost nearly twenty pounds on the trip, but what weight I had left was the bone and sinew of my system, that served me so well on this trip and has been my comfort in other walks of life at a later period. And so, if asked, did you experience hardship on the trip across the plains, I could not answer yes without a mental reservation that it might have been a great deal worse. I say the same as to after experience, for these subsequent fifty years or more of pioneer life, having been blessed with a good constitution, and being now able to say that in the fifty-three years of our married life, the wife has never seen me a day sick in bed. But this is a digression and so we must turn our attention to the trip on the scow, "floating down the river."

In our company, a party of three, a young married couple and an unmarried sister, lounged on their belongings, listlessly watching the ripples on the water, as did also others of the party. But little conversation was passing. Each seemed to be communing with himself or herself, but it was easy to see what were the

thoughts occupying the minds of all. The young husband, it was plain to be seen, would soon complete that
greater journey to the unknown beyond, a condition
that weighed so heavily upon the ladies of the party,
that they could ill conceal their solicitude and sorrow.
Finally, to cheer up the sick husband and brother, the
ladies began in sweet subdued voices to sing the old
familiar song of Home, Sweet Home, whereupon others
of the party joined in the chorus with increased volume
of sound. As the echo of the echo died away, at the
moment of gliding under the shadow of the high mountain, the second verse was begun, but was never finished.
If an electric shock had startled every individual of the
party, there could have been no more simultaneous effect
than when the second line of the second verse was
reached, when instead of song, sobs and outcries of grief
poured forth from all lips. It seemed as if there was a
tumult of despair mingled with prayer pouring forth
without restraint. The rugged boatmen rested upon
their oars in awe, and gave away in smypathy with the
scene before them, until it could be truly said no dry
eyes were left nor aching heart but was relieved. Like
the down pour of a summer shower that suddenly clears
the atmosphere to welcome the bright shining sun that
follows, so this sudden outburst of grief cleared away the
despondency to be replaced by an exalted exhilarating
feeling of buoyancy and hopefulness. The tears were
not dried till mirth took possession—a real hysterical
manifestation of the whole party, that ended all depression for the remainder of the trip.

But our party was not alone in these trials. It seems
to me as like the dream of seeing some immigrants floating on a submerged raft while on this trip. Perhaps, it
is a memory of a memory, or of a long lost story, the
substance remembered, but the source forgotten.

Recently a story was told me by one of the actors
in the drama, that came near a tragic ending. Robert

Parker, who still lives at Sumner, one of the party, has told me of their experience. John Whitacre, afterwards Governor of Oregon, was the head of the party of nine that constructed a raft at The Dalles out of dry poles hauled from the adjacent country. Their stock was then started out over the trail, their two wagons put upon the raft with their provisions, bedding, women, and children in the wagons, and the start was made to float down the river to the Cascades. They had gotten but a few miles until experience warned them. The waves swept over the raft so heavily that it was like a submerged foundation upon which their wagons stood. A landing a few miles out from The Dalles averted a total wreck, and afforded opportunity to strengthen the buoyancy of their raft by extra timber packed upon their backs for long distances. And how should they know when they would reach the falls? Will they be able to discover the falls and then have time to make a landing? Their fears finally got the better of them; a line was run ashore and instead of making a landing, they found themselves hard aground out of reach of land- except by wading a long distance, and yet many miles above the falls (Cascades). Finally, a scow was procured, in which they all reached the head of the Cascades in safety. The old pioneer spoke kindly of this whole party, one might say affectionately. One, a waif picked up on the plains, a tender girl of fifteen, fatherless and motherless, and sick; a wanderer without relatives or acquaintances—all under the sands of the plains—recalled the trials of the trip vividly. But, he had cheerful news of her in after life, though impossible at the moment to recall her name. Such were some of the experiences of the finish of the long, wearisome trip of those who floated down the river on flatboat and raft.

CHAPTER II.

The Arrival.

About nine o'clock at night, with a bright moon shining, on October 1st, 1852, I carried my wife in my arms up the steep bank of the Willamette River, and three blocks away in the town of Portland to a colored man's lodging house.

"Why, sah, I didn't think yuse could do that, yuse don't look it," said my colored friend, as I deposited my charge in the nice, clean bed in a cozy, little room.

From April until October, we had been on the move in the tented field, with never a roof over our heads other than the wagon cover or tent, and for the last three months, no softer bed than either the ground or bottom of the wagon bed. We had found a little steamer to carry us from the Cascades to Portland, with most of the company that had floated down the river from The Dalles, in the great scow. At the landing we separated, and knew each other but slightly afterwards. The great country, Oregon, (then including Puget Sound) was large enough to swallow up a thousand such immigrations and yet individuals be lost to each other, but a sorrier mess it would be difficult to imagine than confronted us upon arrival. Some rain had fallen, and more soon followed. With the stumps and logs, mud and uneven places, it was no easy matter to find a resting place for the tented city so continually enlarging. People seemed to be dazed; did not know what to do; insufficient shelter to house all; work for all impossible; the country looked a veritable great field of forest and mountain. Discouragement and despair seized upon some, while others began to enlarge the circle of observation. A few had friends and acquaintances, which fact began soon to relieve the situation by the removals that followed the reunions, while suffering, both mental and physical, followed the arrival in the winter storm that ensued, yet soon the atmosphere of discontent disappeared, and general cheerfulness prevailed. A few laid down in their beds not to arise again; a few required time to recuperate their strength, but with the majority, a short time found them as active and hearty as if nothing had happened. For myself, I can truly say, I do not remember the experience as a personal hardship. I had been born well of healthy parents. I knew of my father working eighteen hours a day for three years in the Carlisle mill at Indianopolis, Indiana, for 75 cents a day, and as an experienced miller at that. If his iron will or physical perfection or something had enabled him to endure this ordeal and retain his strength, why could not I, thirty years younger, hew my way? I did not feel fatigued. True, I had been "worked down" in flesh, but more from lack of suitable food than from excessive exertion. Any way, I resolved to try.

My brother, Oliver, who had crossed the plains with me—a noble man and one destined, had he lived, to have made his mark—came ahead by the trail. He had spied out the land a little with unsatisfactory results, met me and pointed the way to our colored friend's abode. We divided our purse of $3.75, I retaining two dollars and he taking the remainder, and with earliest dawn of the 2nd found the trail leading down the river, searching for our mutual benefit for something to do.

Did you, reader, ever have the experience of a premonition that led you on to success? Some say this is simply chance; others say that it is a species of superstition, but whatever it is, probably most of us, some time in our lives, have had some sort of trials to set us to thinking.

As we passed up the Willamette, a few miles below Portland, on the evening of our arrival, a bark lay seemingly right in our path as we steamed by. Standing upon the lower deck of our little steamer, this vessel looked to our inexperienced eyes as a veritable monster, with masts reaching to the sky, and hull towering high above our heads. Probably not one of that whole party of frontiersmen had ever before seen a deep sea vessel. Hence, small wonder, the novelty of this great monster, as we all thought of the vessel, should excite our admiration and we might almost say, amazement. That was what we came so far for, to where ships might go down to the sea and return laden with the riches of the earth. The word passed that she was bound for Portland with a cargo of merchandise and to take a return cargo of lumber. There, as we passed, flashed through my mind, will be my opportunity for work tomorrow, on that vessel.

Sure enough, when the morrow came, the staunch bark Mary Melville lay quietly in front of the mill, and so, not losing any time in early morning, my inquiry was made "do you want any men on board this ship?" A gruff looking fellow eyed me all over as much as to say, "not you," but answered, "yes, go below and get your breakfast." I fairly stammered out, I must go and see my wife first, and let her know where I am, whereupon came back a growl "of course, that will be the last of you; that's the way with these new comers, always hunting for work and never wanting it" (this aside to a companion, but in my hearing). I swallowed my indignation with the assurance that I would be back in five minutes and so went post haste to the little sufferer to impart the good news.

Put yourself in my place, you land lubber, who never came under the domination of a brutal mate of a sailing vessel fifty years ago. My ears fairly tingled with hot anger at the harsh orders, but I stuck to the work, smothering my rage at being berated while doing my very best to please and to expedite the work. The fact gradually dawned on me that the man was not angry, but had fallen in the way of talking as though he was, and that the sailors paid slight heed to what he said. Before night, however, the fellow seemed to let up on me, while increasing his tirade on the heads of their regular men. The second and third day wore off with blistered hands, but with never a word about wages or pay.

"Say, boss, I'se got to pay my rent, and wese always gets our pay in advance. I doesn't like to ask you, but can't you get the old boss to put up something on your work?" I could plainly see that it was a notice to pay or move. He was giving it to me in thinly veiled words. What should I do? Suppose the old skipper should take umbrage, and discharge me for asking for wages before the end of the week? But when I told him what I wanted the money for, the old man's eyes moistened, but without a word, he gave me more money than I had asked for, and that night the steward handed me a bottle of wine for the "missus," which I knew instinctively came from the old captain.

The baby's Sunday visit to the ship; the Sunday dinner in the cabin; the presents of delicacies that followed, even from the gruff mate, made me feel that under all this roughness, a tender spot of humanity lay, and that one must not judge by outward appearances too much—that even way out here, three thousand miles from home, the same sort of people lived as those I had left behind me.

"St. Helens, October 7th, 1852.
"Dear Brother: Come as soon as you can. Have rented a house, sixty boarders; this is going to be the place. Shall I send you money?   O. P. M."

The mate importuned me to stay until the cargo was on board, which I did until the last stick of lumber was stowed, the last pig in the pen, and when the ship swung

off bound on her outward voyage, I felt as though I had
an interest in her, but, remembering the forty dollars
in the aggregrate I had received, with most of it to
jingle in my pockets, I certainly could claim no financial
interest, but from that day on I never saw or heard the
name of the bark Mary Melville without pricking my
ears, (figuratively, of course) to hear more about her
and the old captain and his gruff mate.

Sure enough, I found St. Helens to be the place.
Here was to be the terminus of the steamship line from
San Francisco. "Wasn't the company building this
wharf?" They wouldn't set sixty men to work on the
dock without they meant business. "Ships can't get
up that creek" (meaning the Willamette), "the big city
is going to be here." This was the talk that greeted my
ears, after we had carried the wife, (this time in a
chair) to our hotel. Yes, our hotel, and had deposited
her and the baby in the best room the house afforded.

It was here I made acquaintance with Columbia Lancaster, afterwards elected as the first delegate to Congress from Washington. I have always felt that the
published history of those days has not done the old
man justice, and has been governed in part, at least,
by factional bias. Lancaster believed that what was
worth doing at all was worth doing well, and he lived
it. He used to come across the Columbia with his small
boat, rowed by his own hand, laden with vegetables
grown by himself on his farm opposite St. Helens, in
the fertile valley of Lewis River. I soon came to know
that what Lancaster said of his produce was true to the
letter; that if he told me he had good potatoes, he had,
and that they were the same in the middle or bottom of
the sack as at the top. And so with all his produce.
We at once became his heaviest customer, and learned
to trust him implicity. I considered him a typical pioneer, and his name never would have been used so con-
temptuously had it not been that he became a thorn

in the side of men who made politics a trade for personal profit. Lancaster upset their well laid plans, carried off the honors of the democratic nomination, and was elected as our first delegate in Congress from the new Territory of Washington.

One January morning of 1853, the sixty men, (our boarders) did not go to work dock building as usual. Orders had come to suspend work. Nobody knew why, or for how long. We soon learned the why, as the steamship company had given up the fight against Portland, and would thenceforward run their steamers to that port. For how long, was speedily determined, for the dock was not finished and was allowed to fall into decay and disappear by the hand of time.

Our boarders scattered, and our occupation was gone, and our accumulation in great part rendered worthless to us by the change.

Meantime, snow had fallen to a great depth; the price of forage for cattle rose by leaps and bounds, and we found that we must part with half of our stock to save the remainder. It might be necessary to feed for a month, or for three months, but we could not tell, and so the last cow was given up that we might keep one yoke of oxen, so necessary for the work on a new place. Then the hunt for a claim began again. One day's struggle against the current of Lewis River, and a night standing in a snow and sleet storm around a camp fire of green wood, cooled our ardor a little, and two hours sufficed to take us back home next morning.

But claims we must have. That was what we had come to Oregon for; we were going to be farmers. Wife and I had made that bargain before we closed the other more important contract. We were, however, both of one mind as to both contracts. Early in January of 1853 the snow began disappearing rapidly, and the search became more earnest, until finally, about the 20th of

January, I drove my first stake for a claim, to include the site where the town, or city, of Kalama now stands, and here built our first cabin.

That cabin I can see in my mind as vividly as I could the first day after it was finished. It was the first home I ever owned. What a thrill of joy that name brought to us. Home. It was our home, and no one could say aye, yes, or no, as to what we should do. No more rough talk on ship board or at the table; no more restrictions if we wished to be a little closer together. The glow of the cheek had returned to the wife; the dimple to the baby. And such a baby. In the innocence of our souls we really and truly thought we had the smartest, cutest baby on earth. I wonder how many millions of young parents have since experienced that same feeling? I would not tear the veil from off their eyes if I could. Let them think so, for it will do them good—make them happy, even if, perchance, it should be an illusion—it's real to them. But I am admonished that I must close this writing now, and tell about the cabin, and the early garden, and the trip to Puget Sound in another chapter.

CHAPTER III.

The First Cabin.

What a charm the words our first cabin have to the pioneer. To many, it was the first home ever owned by them, while to many others, like myself, the first we ever had. We had been married nearly two years, yet this was really our first abiding place. All others had been merely way stations on the march westward from Indianapolis to this cabin. Built of small, straight logs, on a side hill, with the door in the end fronting the river, and with but little grading, for the rocky nature of the location would not admit of it. Three steps were required to reach the floor. The ribs projected in front a few feet to provide an open front porch, with a ground floor, not for ornament, but for storage for the dry wood and kindling so necessary for the comfort and convenience of the mistress of the house. The walls were but scant five feet, with not a very steep roof, and a large stone fire place and chimney—the latter but seven feet high— completed our first home.

The great river, nearly a mile and three quarters wide, seemed to tire from its ceaseless flow at least once a day as if taking a nooning spell, while the tides from the ocean, sixty miles away, contended for mastery, and sometimes succeeded in turning the current up stream. Immediately in front of our landing lay a small island of a few acres in extent, covered with heavy timber and drift-wood. This has long since disappeared and ships now pass over the spot with safety.

Scarcely had we become settled in our new home before there came a mighty flood that covered the waters of the river with wrecks of property impossible to enumerate. Our attention was immediately turned to securing logs that came floating down the river in great numbers. In a very short time we had a raft that was worth quite a sum of money could we but get it to the market. Encouraged by this find, we immediately turned our attention to some fine timber standing close to the bank near by, and began hand logging to supplement what we had already secured afloat. I have often wondered what we would have done had it not been for this find, for in the course of seven weeks three of us marketed eight hundred dollars worth of logs that enabled us to obtain flour, even if we did pay fifty dollars a barrel, and potatoes at two dollars a bushel, and sometimes more.

And yet, because of that hand logging work, Jane came very near becoming a widow one morning before breakfast, but did not know of it until long afterwards. It occurred in this way. We did not then know how to scaffold up above the tough, swelled butts of the large trees, and this made it very difficult to chop them down. So we burned them by boring two holes at an angle to meet inside the inner bark, and by getting the fire started, the heart of the tree would burn, leaving an outer shell of bark. One morning, as usual, I was up early, and after starting the fire in the stove and putting on the teakettle, I hastened to the burning timber to start afresh the fires, if perchance, some had ceased to burn. Nearing a clump of three giants, two hundred and fifty feet tall, one began toppling over toward me. In my confusion I ran across the path where it fell, and while this had scarce reached the ground, a second started to fall almost parallel to the first, scarcely thirty feet apart at the top, leaving me between the two with limbs flying in a good many directions. If I had not become entangled in some brush, I would have gotten under the last falling tree. It was a marvelous escape, and would almost lead one to think that there is such a thing as a charmed life.

The rafting of our precious accumulations down the Columbia River to Oak Point; the relentless current that carried us by where we had contracted our logs at six dollars a thousand; the following the raft to the larger waters, and finally, to Astoria, where we sold them for eight dollars, instead of six per thousand, thus, profiting by our misfortunes; the involuntary plunge off the raft into the river with my boots on; the three days and nights of ceaseless toil and watching would make a thrilling story if we had but the time to tell it. Our final success was complete, which takes off the keen edge of the excitement of the hour, and when finished, we unanimously voted we would have none of it more.

At Oak Point we found Alexander Abernethy, former Governor of Oregon, who had quite recently returned with his family from the "States," and had settled down in the lumber business. He had a mill running of a capacity of about 25,000 feet of lumber a day. It was a water power mill, and the place presented quite a smart business air for the room they had. But Oak Point did not grow to be much of a lumber or business center, and the water mill eventually gave way to steam, located elsewhere, better suited for the business.

The flour sack was nearly empty when we left home expecting to be absent but one night, and now we had been gone a week. There were no neighbors nearer than four miles and no roads—scarcely a trail—the only communication was by the river. What about the wife and baby alone in the cabin with the deep timber close by in the rear, and heavy jungle of brush in the front? Nothing about it. We found them all right upon our return, but like the log drivers with their experience, the little wife said she wanted no more of cabin life alone. And yet, like adventures and like experiences followed.

The February sun of 1853 shone almost like midsummer. The clearing grew almost as if by magic. We could not resist the temptation to begin planting, and before March was gone, the rows of peas, lettuce, and onions growing on the river bank could be seen from the cabin door, thirty rods away.

One day I noticed some three cornered bits of potatoes that had been cut out, not bigger than the end of my finger. These all ran to a point as though cut out from a pattern. The base, or outer skin, all contained an eye of the potato. The wife said these would grow and would help us out about seed when planting time came, and we could have the body of the potatoes to eat. That would have seemed a plausible scheme had we been able to plant at once, but by this time we had been forcibly reminded that there was another impending flood for June, incident to the melting of the snow on the mountains, a thousand miles away, as the channel ran. But the experiment would not cost much, so the potato eyes were carefully saved and spread out on shelves where they became so dry that they would rattle like dry onion sets when handled. Every steamer outward bound carried potatoes for the San Francisco market, until it became a question whether enough would be left for seed, so that three and even four cents per pound was asked and paid for sorry looking culls. We must have seed, and so, after experimenting with the dried eyes, planted in moist earth in a box kept warm in the cabin, we became convinced that the little lady of the household was right, so ate potatoes freely even at these famine prices. Sure enough, the flood came, the planting delayed until July, and yet a crop was raised that undug brought in nearly four hundred dollars, for we did not stay to harvest them, or in fact, cultivate them, leaving that to another who became interested in the venture.

In April, the word began to pass around that we were

to have a new Terrirtory to embrace the country north of
the Columbia River, with its capital on Puget Sound,
and here on the Columbia we would be way off to one side
and out of touch with the people who would shortly become a great, separate commonwealth. Besides, had we
not come all the way across the plains to get to the *Sea
Board,* and here we were simply on the bank of a river—
a great river to be sure, with its ship channel, but then,
that bar at the mouth, what about it? Then the June
freshet, what about that?

So, one bright morning in May, my brother Oliver
and myself made each of us a pack of forty pounds and
took the trail, bound for Puget Sound, camping where
night overtook us, and sleeping in the open air without
shelter or cover other than that afforded by some
friendly tree with drooping limbs. Our trail first led us
down near the right bank of the Columbia to the Cowlitz, thence up the latter river thirty miles or more, and
then across the country nearly sixty miles to Olympia,
and to the salt sea water of the Pacific sent inland a
hundred and fifty miles by the resistless tides, twice a
day for every day of the year.

Our expectations had been raised by the glowing accounts about Puget Sound, and so, when we could see in
the foreground but bare, dismal mud flats, and beyond
but a few miles of water with a channel scarce twice as
wide as the channel of the great river we had left, bound-
ed on either side by high table, heavily timbered land,
a feeling of deep disappointment fell upon us, with the
wish that we were back at our cabin on the river.

Should we turn around and go back? No, that was
what we had not yet done since leaving our Indiana
home eighteen months before; but what was the use of
stopping here? We wanted a place to make a farm,
and we could not do it on such forbidding land as this.
Had not the little wife and I made a solemn bargain or
compact, before we were married that we were going to

be farmers? Here, I could see a dense forest stretched out before me quite interesting to the lumberman, and for aught I knew, channels for the ships, but I wanted to be neither a lumberman nor sailor, and so, my first camp on Puget Sound was not cheerful and my first night not passed in contentment.

Olympia at the time contained about 100 inhabitants. It could boast having three stores, a hotel, a livery stable, and saloon, with one weekly newspaper, then publishing its thirtieth number. A glance at the advertising columns of this paper, the "Columbian," (named for what was expected would be the name of the new Territory) did not disclose but few local advertisers, the two pages devoted to advertising being filled by announcements of business other than in Olympia. "Everybody knows everybody here," said a business man to me, "so what's the use of advertising?" And it was thus with those who had been in the place for a few weeks, and so it continued all over the pioneer settlements for years. To meet a man on the road or on the street without speaking was considered rude. It became the universal practice to greet even strangers as well as acquaintances, and to this day I doubt if there are many of the old settlers yet devoid of the impulse to pass the time of day with hearty greetings to whomsoever they may meet, be they acquaintances or strangers.

Edmund Sylvester in partnership with Levi L. Smith, located the claims where the town of Olympia is built, in 1848. Mr. Smith soon after died, leaving Sylvester as sole proprietor of the town, where I saw him, as it will appear, five years later. It is said that Colonel I. N. Ebey suggested the name Olympia, which was not given to the place until after Mr. Sylvester's flight to the gold mines of California and return in 1850.

But we could not stay here at Olympia. We had pushed on past some good locations on the Chehalis, and further south, without locating, and now, should we retrace our steps? Brother Oliver said no. My better judgment said no, though sorely pressed with that feeling of homesickness, or blues, or whatever we may call it. The resolve was quickly made that we would see more of this Puget Sound, that we were told presented nearly as many miles of shore line as we had traveled westward from the Missouri River to Portland, near sixteen hundred miles, and which we afterwards found to be true.

But how were we to go and see these, to us unexplored waters? I said I would not go in one of those things, the Indian canoe, that we would upset it before we were out half an hour. Brother Oliver pointed to the fact the Indians navigated the whole Sound in these canoes, and were safe, but I was inexorable and would not trust my carcass in a craft that would tip so easily as a Siwash canoe. When I came to know the Indians better, I ceased to use such a term, and afterwards when I saw the performances of these apparently frail craft, my admiration was greater in degree than my contempt had been.

Of the cruise that followed on Puget Sound, and in what manner of craft we made it, and of various incidents of the trip that occupied a month, I must defer telling now, and leave this part of the story for succeeding chapters.

CHAPTER IV.

Cruise on Puget Sound.

Put yourself in my place, reader, for a time—long enough to read this chapter. Think of yourself as young again, if elderly (I will not say old) ; play you have been old and now young again, until you find out about this trip on Puget Sound fifty and more years ago. Then think of Puget Sound in an inquiring mood, as though you knew nothing about it, only a little indefinite hear-say ; enough to know there is such a name, but not what manner of place or how large or how small ; whether it was one single channel, like a river, or numerous chan-nels ; whether it was a bay or a series of bays or whether it was a lake, but somehow connected with the sea, and then you will be in the mood these two young men were, when they descended the hill with their packs on their backs and entered the town of Olympia in May, 1853. Now, if you are in this inquiring mood, I will take you in my confidence and we will live the cruise over again of thirty-two days of adventures and observation on Puget Sound fifty years ago.

I was but a few months past twenty-three, while my brother Oliver could claim nearly two years seniority. We had always played together as boys, worked together as men, and lived together even after his marriage until the day of his death, now forty-five years ago, and so far as I can remember, never had a disagreement in our whole life.

So, when we cast off the line at Olympia, on or about the 28th day of May, 1853, we were assured of one thing and that was a concert of action, be there danger or only labor ahead. Neither of us had had much experience in boating, and none as to boat building, but when we decided to make the trip and discarded the idea of taking a canoe we set to work with a hearty good will to build us a skiff out of light lumber, then easily obtained at the Tumwater mill of Hays, Ward & Co., in business at that place.

I knew Ira Ward of the firm of Hays & Ward intimately for long years afterwards and I may say until the day of his death which recently occurred at the advanced age of 86 years, and can testify as to his worth as a citizen of the new commonwealth where he cast his lot and to his kindly nature with an unbounded hospitality to which so many of the early pioneers can testify.

We determined to have the skiff broad enough to not upset easily, and long enough to carry us and our light cargo of food and bedding. Like the trip across the plains we must provide our own transportation. We were told that the Sound was a solitude so far as transportation facilities, with here and there a vessel loading piles and square timber for the San Francisco market. Not a steamer was then plying on the Sound; not even a sailing craft that essayed to carry passengers. We did not really know whether we would go twenty miles or a hundred; whether we would find small waters or large; straight channels or intricate by-ways; in a word we knew but very little of what lay before us. If we had known a little more, we would not have encountered the risks we did. One thing we knew, we could endure sturdy labor without fatigue, and improvised camp without discomfort, for we were used to just such experiences. Poor innocent souls, we thought we could follow the shore line and thus avoid danger, and perhaps float with the tide, and thus minimize the labor, and yet keep our bearings.

George A. Barnes sold us the nails and oakum for

building the boat and charged us 25 cents per pound for the former, but he could not sell us any pitch as that was to be had for the taking. However, articles of merchandise were not high, though country produce sold for extreme prices.

Recently I have seen a "retail prices current of Puget Sound, Washington Territory, corrected weekly by Parker, Colter & Co.," in which, among many others, the following prices are quoted in the columns of the only paper in the Territory then published in Olympia, the "Columbian," as follows:

Pork, per lb	$ .20
Flour, per 100 lbs	10.00
Potatoes, per bushel	3.00
Butter, per lb	1.00
Onions, per bushel	4.00
Eggs, per dozen	1.00
Beets, per bushel	3.50
Sugar, per lb	.12½
Coffee, per lb	.18
Tea, per lb	75c and 1.00
Molasses, per gallon	50 and .75
Salmon, per lb	.10
Whisky, per gallon	1.00
Sawed lumber, fir, per M	20.00
Cedar, per M	30.00
Shingles,, per M	$4.25 to 5.00
Piles, per foot	5 to .08
Square timber, per foot	12 to .15

Thus it will be seen that what the farmer had to sell was high while much he must buy was comparatively cheap, even his whisky, then but a dollar a gallon, while his potatoes sold for $3.00 a bushel.

This Parker, of Parker, Colter & Co., is the same John G. Parker, Jr., of steamboat fame who yet lives in Olympia, now an old man, but never contented without his hand on the wheel in the pilot house, where I saw him but a few months ago on his new steamer the Caswell, successor to his first, the Traveler, of fifty years before.

Two or three other stores besides Barnes' and Parker's were then doing business in Olympia, the Kandall Company, with Joseph Cushman as agent; A. J. Moses, and I think the Bettman Brothers.

Rev. Benjamin F. Close, Methodist, held religious service in a small building near Barnes' store, but there was no church edifice for several years. Near by, the saloon element had found a foothold, but I made no note of them in my mind other than to remember they were there and running every day of the week including Sunday.

The townsite proprietor, Edmund Sylvester, kept the hotel of the town, the "Washington," at the corner of 2nd and Main Street, a locality now held to be too far down on the water front, but then the center of trade and traffic.

G. N. McConaha and J. W. Wiley dispensed the law and H. A. Goldsborough & Simmons (M. T. Simmons) looked out for the real estate and conveyances. Add to these a bakery, a livery stable, and a blacksmith shop and we have the town of Olympia in our mind again of possibly 100 people who then believed a great future lay in store for their embryo city "at the head of Puget Sound."

Three leading questions occupied the attention of all parties while we were in this little ambitious city, the new Territorial organization so soon to be inaugurated, the question of an overland railroad, and of an over mountain immigrant wagon road. The last was the absorbing topic of conversation, as it was a live enterprise dependent upon the efforts of the citizens for success. Meetings had been held in different parts of the district west of the Cascade Mountains and north of the Columbia River, and finally subscription lists were circulated, a cashier and superintendent appointed, with the result, as stated elsewhere, of opening the way for the first immigration over the Cascade Mountains via the Natchess Pass, but the particulars of this work are given in other chapters following.

As the tide drew off the placid waters of the bay at Olympia with just a breath of air, our little craft behaved splendidly as the slight ripples were jostled against the bow under the pressure of the sail and brought dreams of a pleasure trip, to make amends for the tiresome pack across the country. Nothing can be more enjoyable than favorable conditions in a boating trip, the more especially to those who have long been in the harness of severe labor, and for a season must enjoy enforced repose. And so we lazily floated with the tide, sometimes taking a few strokes with the oars, and at other times whistling for the wind, as the little town of Olympia to the south, became dimmed by distance.

At this southern extremity of the Sound without the accumulations of water to struggle for passage, as through the channel to the north, the movement is neither swift, nor disturbed with cross currents to agitate the surface—more like the steady flow of a great river.

But we were no sooner fairly out of sight of the little village and out of the bay it was situated upon (Budd's Inlet), than the query came up as to which way to go. Was it this channel or that or yet another one we should take? Let the tide decide; that will take us out toward the ocean we urged. No, we are drifting into another bay; that cannot be where we want to go; why, we are drifting right back almost in the same direction from which we came, but into another bay. We'll pull this way to that point to the northeast. But there seems a greater opening of waters to the northwest; yes, but I do not see any way out there. Neither is there beyond that point (Johnson's Point); and so we talked and pulled and puzzled until finally it dawned upon us that the tide had turned and we were being carried back to almost the spot from whence we came, into South bay.

"Now the very best thing we can do is to camp," said the senior of the party of two, to which the junior, your humble writer, readily assented, and so our first night's camp was scarcely twelve miles from where we had started in the morning.

What a nice camping place this. The ladies would say lovely, and why not? A beautiful pebbly beach that extended almost to the water's edge even at low tide with a nice grassy level spit; a back ground of evergreen giant fir timber; such clear cool water gushing out from the bank near by, so superlative in quality as to defy word to adequately describe; and such fuel for the camp fire, broken fir limbs with just enough pitch to make a cheerful blaze and yet body enough to last well. Why, we felt so happy that we were almost glad the journey had been interrupted. Oliver was the carpenter of the party, the tent builder, wood getter, and general roust-a-bout, to coin a word from camp parlance, while I, the junior, was the "chief cook and bottle washer," as the senior would jocularly put it.

At the point a little beyond where we landed we found next morning J. R. Johnson, M. D., with his cabin on the point under the pretentious name of "Johnson's Hospital," opened as he said for the benefit of the sick, but which, from what I saw in my later trips think his greatest business was in disposing of cheap whisky of which he contributed his share of the patronage.

An Indian encampment being near by, a party of them soon visited our camp and began making signs for trade. "*Mika tik-eh clams?*" came from out the mouth of one of the matrons of the party as if though half choked in the speaking, a cross between a spoken word and a smothered gutteral sound in the throat.

"What does she say, Oliver?" the junior said, turning for counsel to the superior wisdom of the elder brother.

"I'm blessed if I know what she says, but she evidently wants to sell some clams."

And so, after considerable dickering, and by signs and gestures and words oft repeated we were able to impart the information that we wanted a lesson in cookery; that we wanted her to show us how to cook them, and that we would buy some. This brought some merriment in the camp. The idea, that there lived a person that did not know how to cook clams. Without saying by your leave or any thing else the motherly looking native began tearing down our camp fire.

"Let her alone," said the senior, "and see what she's up to," noticing that the younger man was going to remonstrate against such an interference with his well laid plans for bread baking. And so the kitchen of the camp was surrendered to the native matron, who quietly covered the hot pebbles and sand where the fire had been, with a light layer of pebbles, upon which the clams were deposited and some fine twigs placed on top, upon which earth was deposited. "*K-l-o-s-h-e*," said the matron. "*Hy-as-kloshe*," said her seignior, who sat squatting watching the operation with evident pride upon the achievement of his dame.

"What did they say?" innocently inquired the junior brother.

"I know what they said, but I don't know what they meant," responded the elder one, "unless it was she had done a good job, which I think she has," and thus began and ended our first lesson in the Chinook jargon, and our first introduction to a clam bake.

What memories hover around these three words, "the clam bake." Did you ever, may I ask my readers, other than those of ye olden times, did you ever participate in the joys of a regular old-fashioned clam bake, with or without the corn, with or without the help of the deft native hand? If you never have, then go straighway, before you die, to the end that you may ever after have the memory of the first clam bake, even if it be but a memory, and likewise be the last.

Our first clam bake gave us great encouragement. We soon learned that these bivalves were to be found in almost unlimited quantity, and were widely distributed; that the harvest was ready twice a day, when the tide was out, and that we need have no fear of a famine even if cast away in some unfrequented place.

"*Yah-ka kloshe al-ta,*" said the dame, uncovering the steaming mass and placing them on a sliver found near by, "*de-late kloshe; kloshe muck-a-muck alt-ta,*" and so, without understanding what she said, but knowing well what she meant, we fell to in disposing of this, our first clam dinner.

Dividing with them the bread that had been baked, and some potatoes that had been boiled, the natives soon withdrew to their own camp, where, before retiring for the night, we repaid the visit.

To see the little fellows of the camp scud behind the mother when the strangers entered, and shyly peep out from their retreat, and the mother lovingly reassuring them with kind, affectionate caresses, and finally coaxing them out from under cover, revealed the character of the natives we had neither of us realized before. We had been in the Indian country for nearly a year, but with guns by our sides if not in our hands for nearly half the time, while on the plains, but we had not stopped to study the Indian character. We took it for granted that the Indians were our enemies and watched them suspiciously accordingly, but here seemed to be a disposition manifested to be neighborly and helpful. We took a lesson in Chinook, and by signs and words combined held conversation until a late hour, when, upon getting ready for taking leave, a slice of venison was handed us, sufficient for several meals. Upon offering to pay for it we were met with a shake of the head, and with the words, "*wake, wake, kul-tus-pot-latch,*" which we understood by their actions to mean they made us a present of it.

This present from the Indian let in a flood of light upon the Indian character. We had made them a present first, it was true, but we did not expect any return, except perhaps good will, and in fact, cannot now say we particularly expected that, but were impelled to do our act of courtesy from the manner of their treatment and from the evident desire to be on friendly terms. From that time on during the trip, and I may say, for all time since, I have found the Indians of Puget Sound ready to reciprocate acts of kindness, and hold in high esteem a favor granted if not accompanied by acts apparently designed to simply gain an advantage.

We often forget the sharp eyes and ears of little children and let slip words that are quickly absorbed to their hurt by affecting their conduct. While the Indian is really not a suspicious person, nevertheless, he is quick to detect and as quick to resent a real or supposed slight as the little five year old who discovers his elders in their fibs or deceit. Not that the Indian expects socially to be received in your house or at your table, yet little acts of kindness, if done without apparent design, touch their better nature and are repaid more than a hundred fold, for you thereafter have a friend and neighbor, and not an enemy or suspicious maligner.

All of this did not dawn on the young men at the time, though their treatment of the Indians was in harmony with friendly feelings which we found everywhere and made a lasting impression.

Subsequent experience, of course, has confirmed these first impressions with the wider field of observation in after years, while employing large numbers of these people in the hop fields of which I hope to write later. And so now must end this chapter with the subject of the "cruise" to be continued at another sitting.

CHAPTER V.

Cruise on Puget Sound—Continued.

"Keep to the right, as the law directs," is an old western adage that governs travelers on the road, but we kept to the right because we wanted to follow the shore, as we thought it safer, and besides, why not go that way as well as any other,—it was all new to us. So, on the second morning, as we rounded Johnson's Point and saw no channel opening in any direction; saw only water in the foreground and timber beyond, we concluded to skirt the coast line and see what the day would bring forth. This led us a southeasterly course and in part doubling back with that traveled the previous day, and past what became the historic grounds of the Medicine Creek Treaty council, or, rather leaving this two miles to our right as the Nisqually flats were encountered. Here we were crowded to a northerly course leaving the Nisqually House on the beach to the east without stopping for investigation.

According to Finlayson's journal, as I afterwards ascertained, this had been built twenty-three years before. At least, some house had been built on this spot at that time, (1829 or 1830) though the fort by that name one fourth mile back from the water was not constructed until the summer of 1833, just twenty years previous to our visit.

This fort mentioned must not be confounded with the Nisqually fort built some three years later (1836) a mile farther east and convenient to the waters of Segwalitchew creek, which there runs near the surface of the surrounding country. All remains of the old fort have long since vanished, but the nearly filled trenches where the stockade timbers stood can yet be traced, showing that a space 250 feet square had been enclosed. Another visible sign was an apple tree yet alive near the spot, grown from seed planted in 1833, but now, when I visited the place in June, 1903, overshadowed by a lusty fir that is sapping the life of the only living, though mute, witness (except it may be the Indian, Steilacoom) we have of those early days, when the first fort was built by the intrepid employes of the Hudson Bay Company.

An interesting feature of the intervening space between the old and the newer fort is the dense growth of fir timber averaging nearly two feet in diameter and in some cases fully three, and over a hundred feet high on what was prairie when the early fort builders began work. The land upon which this timber is growing still shows unmistakable signs of the furrow marks that can be traced through the forest. Verily, this *is* a most wonderful country where forest product will grow, if properly protected, more rapidly than the hand of man will destroy.

As the tide and wind favored us we did not stop, but had not proceeded far before we came in sight of a fleet of seven vessels lying at anchor in a large bay of several miles in extent.

Upon the eastern slope of the shores of this bay lay the two towns, Port Steilacoom, established January 23rd, 1851, by Captain Lafayette Balch and Steilacoom City, upon an adjoining land claim taken by John B. Chapman, August 23rd, of same year and later held by his son John M. Chapman. These two rival towns were built, as far apart as possible on the frontage lands of the claim owners (about one mile apart) and became known locally as Upper and Lower Steilacoom, the latter name being applied to Balch's town.

We found the stocks of goods carried by the merchants of these two towns exceeded those held by the

Olympia merchants, and that at Fort Nisqually, six miles distant, the merchandise carried by the Puget Sound Agricultural Company would probably equal that of all three of the towns combined, possibly, in the aggregate, over one hundred thousand dollars for the whole district under review.

Evidently a far larger trade centered on Steilacoom Bay and vicinity than at any other point we had seen and, as we found afterwards, than any other point on Puget Sound. Naturally we would here call a halt to examine the country and to make ourselves acquainted with the surroundings that made this early center of trade.

One mile and a half back from the shore and east of lower Steilacoom, we found what was by courtesy called Fort Steilacoom, but which was simply a camp of a company of United States soldiers, in wooden shells of houses and log cabins. This camp, or fort, had been established by Captain Bennett H. Hill with Company M, 1st Artillery, August 27th, 1849, following the attempted robbery of Fort Nisqually the previous May by Pat Kanim and his followers, the Snoqualmie Indians.

Dr. Tolmie, Chief Factor of the Puget Sound Agricultural Company at Fort Nisqually, quickly seized the opportunity to demand rent from the United States for the occupancy of the site of Fort Steilacoom of six hundred dollars a year, and actually received it for fifteen years and until the final award was made extinguishing the claims of his company. We found the plains alive with this company's stock (many thousand head) running at large and fattened upon the scant but nutritious grass growing upon the adjacent prairie and glade lands.

Balch and Webber were driving a thriving trade in their store at the little town of Steilacoom, besides their shipping trade of piles and square timber, shingles, lumber, cord wood, hides, furs, fish, and other odds and ends. Just across the street from their store stood the main hotel of the place with the unique history of being the only building erected on Puget Sound from lumber shipped from the eastern seaboard. Captain Balch brought the building with him from Maine, ready to set up. At the upper town Philip Keach was merchandising while Abner Martin kept a hotel. Intense rivalry ran between the two towns in the early days when we were at Steilacoom.

Thomas M. Chambers, father of the prominent members of the Olympia community of that name, had built a saw-mill on Steilacoom creek, two miles from the town and a grist mill where farmers oftentimes came with pebbles in their wheat to dull the burrs.

We are wont now to speak of this place as "poor old Steilacoom," with its tumbled-down houses, rotting sidewalks and decayed wharves, the last vestige of the latter of which has disappeared; but then everything was new, with an air of business bustle that made one feel here was a center of trade. The sight of those seven vessels lying in the offing made a profound impression upon our minds. We had never before seen so many ships at one place as were quietly lying at anchor in front of the embryo city. Curiously enough, here was the very identical vessel we had first seen on the Willamette River, the bark "Mary Melville," with her gruff mate and the big hearted master, Capt. Barston, with whom the reader has been made acquainted in a previous chapter. I took no special note of the names of these vessels other than this one, but from the columns of the Columbian I am able to glean the names of twenty-two vessels, brigs, barks, and schooners, then plying between Puget Sound and San Francisco, which are as follows:

Brig Cyclops, Perkins; Bark Delegate, ———; Brig Tarquina, ———; Bark John Adams, McKelmer; Brig G. W. Kendall, Gove; Brig Merchantman, Bolton;

Brig Kingsbury, Cook; Schooner Cynosure, Fowler; Brig George Emery, Diggs; Bark Mary Melville, Barston; Bark Brontes, Blinn; Bark Sarah Warren, Gove; Ship Persia, Brown; Brig I. C. Cabot, Dryden; Brig Jane, Willett; Ship Rowena, ————; Brig Willingsly, Gibbs; Brig Mary Dare, Mowatt; Brig John Davis, Pray; Bark Carib, Plummer; Brig Leonesa, Howard; and Schooner Franklin, Leary. There were probably more, but I do not recall them, but these were enough to keep every man busy that could swing an axe, drag a saw or handle that instrument of torture, the goad stick, and who was willing to work.

All this activity came from the shipment of piles, square timbers, cordwood, shingles, with small quantities of lumber—all that was obtainable, which was not very much, to the San Francisco market. The descent of timber on the roll-ways sounded like distant thunder, and could be heard almost all hours of the day, even where no camps were in sight, but lay hidden up some secluded bay or inlet.

We were sorely tempted to accept the flattering offer of $4.00 each per day for common labor in a timber camp, but soon concluded not to be swerved from the course we had outlined.

It was here, and I think at this time, I saw the Indian "Steilacoom" who still lives. I saw him recently at his camp in the Nisqually bottom, and judge he is bordering on ninety years. Steilacoom helped to build old Fort Nisqually in 1833, and was a married man at that time. People called him chief because he happened to bear the name adopted for the town and creek, but he was not a man of much force of character and not much of a chief. I think this is a remarkable case of longevity for an Indian. As a race, they are short lived. It was here, and during this visit, we began seeing Indians in considerable numbers. Off the mouth of the Nisqually and several places along the beach and floating on the bay we saw several hundred in the aggregrate of all ages and kind. There seemed to be a perfect abandon as to care or thought for the future, or even as to the immediate present, literally floating with the tide. In those days, the Indians seemed to work or play by spurts and spells. Here and there that day a family might be seen industriously pursuing some object, but as a class there seemed to be but little life in them, and we concluded they were the laziest set on earth. I afterwards materially modified that opinion, as I became better acquainted with their habits, for I have found just as industrious Indians, both men and women, and as reliable workers, as among the whites though this class, it may be said, is exceptional with the men. The women are all industrious.

Shall we camp here and spy out the land, or shall we go forward and see what lay before us? Here were the ideals, that had enticed us so far from our old home, where "ships went down into the sea," with the trade of the whole world before us. We waxed eloquent, catching inspiration from people of the town. After a second sober thought we found we had nothing to trade but labor, and we had not come this far to be laborers for hire. We had come to look up a place to make a farm and a farm we were going to have. We, therefore set about searching for claims, and the more we searched the less we liked the looks of things.

The gravelly plains near Steilacoom would not do; neither the heavy fir timber lands skirting the waters of the Sound, and we were nonplussed and almost ready to condemn the country. Finally, on the fourth day after a long, wearisome tramp, we cast off at high tide, and in a dead calm, to continue our cruise. The senior soon dropped into a comfortable afternoon nap, leaving me in full command. As the sun shone nice and warm and the tide was taking us rapidly in the direction we wanted to go, why not join, even if we did lose the sight seeing for which the journey was made.

I was shortly after aroused by the senior exclaiming, "What is that?" and then answering half to himself and half to me, "Why, as I live, it's a deer swimming way out here in the bay." Answering, half asleep and half awake, that that could not be, the senior said: "Well, that's what it is." We gave chase and soon succeeded in getting a rope over its horns. We had by this time drifted into the Narrows, and soon found that we had something more important to look after than towing a deer among the tide-rips of the Sound, and turning him loose pulled for dear life for the shore, and found shelter in an eddy. A perpendicular bluff rose from the high water mark, leaving no place for a camp fire or bed. The tide seemed to roll in waves and with contending forces of currents, and counter currents, yet all moving in a general direction. It was our first introduction to a real genuine, live tide-rip, that seemed to harry the waters as if boiling in a veritable caldron, swelling up here and there in centers to whirl in dizzy velocity and at times break into a foam, and, where a light breeze prevailed, into spray. Then in some areas would seem the waters in solid volume would leap up in conical, or pointed shape—small waves broken into short sections, that would make it quite difficult for a flat bottom boat like our little skiff to float very long. We congratulated ourselves upon the escape, while belittling our careless imitation of the natives of floating with the tide. Just then some Indian canoes passed along moving with the tide. We expected to see them swamped as they encountered the troubled waters, but to our astonishment they passed right through without taking a drop of water. Then here came two well manned canoes creeping along shore against the tide. I have said well-manned, but in fact, half the paddles were wielded by women, and the post of honor, or that where most dexterity was required, was occupied by a woman.   In shore, short eddies would favor the party, to be ended by a severe tug against the stiff current.

"*Me-si-ka-kwass kopa s'kookum chuck,*" said the maiden in the bow of the first canoe, as it drew along side our boat, in which we were sitting.

Since our evening's experience at the clam bake camp, we had been industriously studying language, and pretty well mastered the chinook, and so we with but little difficulty understood her to ask if we were afraid of the rough waters, to which we responded, part in English and part in Chinook, that we were, and besides that it was impossible for us to proceed against the strong current.

"*Ne-si-ka mit-lite,*" that is to say, she said they were going to camp with us and wait for the turn of the tide, and accordingly landed near by, and so we must wait for the remainder of this story in chapters to follow.

CHAPTER VI.

Cruise on Puget Sound—Continued.

By the time the tide had turned, night had come and we were in a quandary as to what to do; whether to camp in our boat, or to start out on unknown waters in the dark. Our Indian visitors began making preparations to proceed on their journey, and assured us it was all right ahead, and offered to show us the way to good camping grounds in a big bay where the current was not strong, and where we would find a great number of Indians in camp.

It did not occur to us to have any fear of the Indians. We did not at all depend on our prowess or personal courage, but felt that we were among friends. We had by this time come to know the general feeling existing between Indians and whites, and that there were no trouble, as a class, whatever there might be as to individuals. I do not want my reader to understand we thought we were doing an heroic act in following a strange party of Indians into unknown waters and into an unknown camp of the natives after dark, or that I think so now. There was no danger ahead of us other than that incident to the attempt of navigating such waters with so frail a boat, and one so unsuited in shape as well as build, for rough waters, and by persons so inexperienced on the water.

Sure enough, a short pull with a favorable current, brought us through the Narrows and into Commencement Bay and in sight of numerous camp fires in the distance. Our Indian friends lazily paddled along in company, while we labored vigorously with our oars as we were by this time in a mood to find a camp where we could have a fire and prepare some food. I remember that camp quite vividly, though cannot locate it exactly, but know that it was on the water front within the present limits of the City of Tacoma. A beautiful small rivulet came down a ravine and spread out on the beach, and I can remember the shore line was not precipitous and that it was a splendid camping ground. The particular thing I do remember is our supper of fresh salmon. Of all the delicious fish known, give me the salmon caught by trolling in early summer in the deep waters of Puget Sound; so fat that the excess of oil must be turned out of the pan while cooking. We had not then learned the art of cooking on the spit, or at least, did not practice it. We had scarcely gotten our camp fire under way before a salmon was offered us, but I cannot recall what we paid, but I know it was not a high price, else we would not have purchased. At the time we did not know but trolling in deep water for this king of fish was the only way, but afterwards learned of the enormous quantities taken by the seine direct from salt water.

Two gentlemen, Messrs. Swan and Riley, had established themselves on the bay, and later in the season reported taking two thousand large fish at one haul with their seine, three fourths of which were salmon. As I have a fish story of my own to tell of our experience later, I will dismiss the subject for the present.

We were now in the bay, since made famous in history by that observing traveler, Theodore Winthrop, who came from the north a few months later and saw that great mountain, that "cloud compeller," reflected in the

TACOMA HARBOR, 1853.

placid waters of the Sound, "Tacoma"* as he wrote,
Rainier, as we saw it. A beautiful sight it was and
is, whatever the name, but to us it was whatever others
said it was, while Winthrop, of a poetic mind, was on
the alert for something new under the sun, if it be no
more than a name for a great mountain.*

Winthrop came in September, while we were in the
bay in June, thus ante-dating his trip by three months
or more. To Winthrop belongs the honor of originating
the name Tacoma from some word claimed to have been
spoken by the Indians as the name of the mountain.
As none of the pioneers ever heard the word until many
years afterwards, and not then until after the post-
humous publication of Winthrop's works ten years after
his visit, I incline to the opinion that Winthrop coined
the word out of his imaginative brain.

We again caught sight of the mountain the next day,
as we approached the tide flats off the mouth of the
Puyallup River. We viewed the mountain with awe
and admiration, but gave no special heed to it, more than
to many other new scenes engaging our attention. It
was land we wanted whereby we might stake a claim,
and not scenery to tickle our fancy. Yet, I doubt if there

---

*Winthrop, in his delightful book, "The Canoe and the Saddle," describing
his trip from Port Townsend to Nisqually, in September, 1853, says:

"We had rounded a point and opened Puyallop Bay, a breath of sheltered
calmness, when I, lifting sleepy eyelids for a dreamy stare about, was suddenly aware of a vast white shadow in the water. What cloud, piled mas-
sive on the horizon, could cast an image so sharp in outline, so full of vigorous detail of surface? No cloud, as my stare, no longer dreamy, presently
discovered—no cloud, but a cloud compeller. It was a giant mountain dome
of snow, swelling and seeming to fill the aerial spheres as its image displaced
the blue deeps of tranquil water. The smoky haze of an Oregon August hid
all the length of its lesser ridges, and left this mighty summit based upon
uplifting dimness. Only its splendid snows were visible, high in the un-
earthly regions of blue noonday sky. The shore line drew a cincture of pines
across its broad base, where it faded unreal into the mist. The same dark
girth separated the peak from its reflection, over which my canoe was now
pressing, and sending wavering swells to scatter the beautiful vision before it.

"Kingly and alone stood this majesty, without any visible consort, though
far to the north and to the south its brethren and sisters dominated their
realms, each in isolated sovereignty, rising from the pine-darkened sierra of
the Cascade Mountains—above the stern chasm where the Columbia, Achilles
of rivers, sweeps, short lived and jubilant, to the sea—above the lovely valley
of the Willamette and Ningua. Of all the peaks from California to Frazier
River, this one was royalest. Mount Regnier, Christians have dubbed it in
stupid nomenclature, perpetuating the name of somebody or nobody. More
melodiously the Siwashes call it Tacoma—a generic term, also applied to all
snow peaks."

lives a man, or ever did, who has seen that great mountain, but has been inspired with higher thoughts, and we may say higher aspirations, or who has ever tired looking upon this grand pile, the father of five great rivers.

We floated into the mouth of the Puyallup River with a vague feeling as to its value, but did not proceed far until we were interrupted by a solid drift of monster trees and logs, extending from bank to bank up the river for a quarter of a mile or more. We were told by the Indians there were two other like obstructions a few miles farther up the river, and that the current was "*de-late-hyas-skoo-kum*," which interpreted means that the current was *very* strong. We found this to be literally true during the next two or three days we spent on the river.

We secured the services of an Indian and his canoe to help us up the river, and left our boat at the Indian's camp near the mouth.

The tug of two days to get six miles up the river, the unloading of our outfit three times to pack it over cut-off trails, and the dragging of our canoe around the drifts, is a story of constant toil with consequent discouragement, not ending until we camped on the bank of the river within the present limits of the little thriving city of Puyallup, founded afterwards by me on a homestead claim taken many years later. The little city now contains nearly four thousand inhabitants, and is destined to contain many thousand more in the lapse of time.

The Puyallup valley at that time was a solitude. No white settlers were found, though it was known two, who lived with Indian women, had staked claims and made some slight improvements—a man by the name of Hayward, near where the town of Sumner is now located, and William Benson, on the opposite side of the river, and a mile distant from the boundaries of Puyallup. An Indian trail led up the river from Commencement Bay, and one westward to the Nisqually plains, over which pack animals could pass, but as to wagon roads, there were none, and as to whether a feasible route for one could be found only time with much labor could determine.

When we retraced our steps, and on the evening of the third day landed again at the mouth of the river after a severe day's toil of packing around drifts and hauling the canoe overland past drifts, it was evident we were in no cheerful mood. Oliver did not sing as usual while preparing for camp, or rally with sallies of wit and humor as he was wont to do when in a happy mood. Neither did I have much to say, but fell to work mechanically preparing the much needed meal, which we ate in silence, and forthwith wrapped ourselves in our blankets for the night, but not for immediate slumber.

We had crossed the two great states of Illinois and Iowa, over hundreds of miles of unoccupied prairie land as rich as anything that "ever laid out of doors," on our way from Indiana to Oregon, in search of land on which to make a home, and here, at what we might say "at the end of our rope" had found the land, but under such adverse conditions that seemed almost too much to overcome. It was a discouraging outlook, even if there had been roads. Such timber! It seemed an appalling undertaking to clear it, the greater portion being covered with a heavy growth of balm and alder trees, and thick tangle of underbrush besides, and so, when we did fall to sleep that night, it was without visions of new found wealth.

And yet, later, I did tackle a quarter section of that heaviest timber land, and never let up until the last tree, log, stump, and root disappeared, though of course, not all of it by my own hands. Nevertheless, with a goodly part, I did say come, boys, and went into the thickest of the work.

But, of the time of which I am writing, there were more to consider than the mere clearing, which we estimated would take thirteen years of solid work for one man to clear a quarter section; the question of going where absolutely there were no neighbors, no roads, no help to open them, and in fact, without a knowledge as to whether a feasible route could be found, compelled us to decide against locating.

A small factor came in to be considered. Such swarms of mosquitoes we had never seen before. These we felt would make life a burden, forgetting that as the country became opened they would disappear. I may relate here a curious phenomenon brought to light by after experience. My donation claim was finally located on high table land, where no surface water could be found in summer for miles around, and there were swarms of mosquitoes, while on the Puyallup homestead taken later, six miles from the mouth of the river, and where water lay on the surface, in spots, the whole summer long, we seldom saw one of these pests there. I never could account for this, and have long since ceased to try; I only know it was so.

If we could have but known what was coming four months later, I doubt not, notwithstanding our discouragement, we would have remained and searched the valley diligently for the choicest locations. In October following, there came the first immigrants that ever crossed the Cascade Mountains, and located in a body nearly all of the whole valley, and before the year was ended had a rough wagon road out to the prairies and to Steilacoom, the county seat.

As I will give an account of the struggles and trials of these people later in this work, I will here dismiss the subject by saying that no pioneer who settled in the Puyallup valley, and stuck to it, failed finally to prosper and gain a competence.

We lingered at the mouth of the river in doubt as to what best to do. My thoughts went back to the wife and baby in the lonely cabin on the Columbia River, and then again to that bargain we had made before marriage that we were going to be farmers, and how could we be farmers if we did not have the land? Under the donation act we could hold three hundred and twenty acres, but we must live on it for four years, and so it behooved us to look out and secure our location before the act expired, which would occur the following year. So, with misgivings and doubts, we finally, on the fourth day, loaded our outfit into our skiff and floated out on the receding tide, whither, we did not know.

CHAPTER VII.

Cruise on Puget Sound—Continued.

As we drew off on the tide from the mouth of the Puyallup River, numerous parties of Indians were in sight, some trolling for salmon, with a lone Indian in the bow of his canoe, others with a pole with barbs on two sides fishing for smelt, and used in place of a paddle, while again, others with nets, all leisurely pursuing their calling, or more accurately speaking, seemed waiting for a fisherman's luck. Again, other parties were passing, singing a plaintive ditty in minor key with two or more voices, accompanied by heavy stroke of the paddle handle against the side of the canoe, as if to keep time. There were really some splendid female voices to be heard, as well as male, and though there were but slight variations in the sounds or words, they seemed never to tire in repeating, and, I must confess, we never tired listening. Then, at times, a break in the singing would be followed by a hearty laugh, or perhaps a salutation be given in a loud tone to some distant party, which would always bring a response, and with the resumption of the paddles, like the sailors on the block and fall, the song would be renewed, oftentimes to bring back a distant echo from a bold shore. These scenes were repeated time and again, as we encountered the natives in new fields that constantly opened up to our view.

We laid our course in the direction the tide drew us, directly to the north in a channel three miles in width, and discarded the plan of following the shore line, as we found so little variation in the quality of soil. By this time we began to see that opportunities for farms on the immediate shores of Puget Sound were few and far between—in fact, we had seen none. During the afternoon and after we had traveled, by estimate, near twenty miles, we saw ahead of us larger waters, where, by continuing our course, we would be in a bay of five or six miles in width, with no very certain prospect of a camping place. Just then we spied a cluster of cabins and houses on the point to the east, and made a landing at what proved to be Alki Point, the place then bearing the pretentious name of New York.

We were not any too soon in effecting our landing, as the tide had turned and a slight breeze had met it, the two together disturbing the water in a manner to make it uncomfortable for us in our flat bottomed boat.

Here we met the irrepressible C. C. Terry, proprietor of the new townsite, but keenly alive to the importance of adding to the population of his new town. But we were not hunting townsites, and of course lent a deaf ear to the arguments set forth in favor of the place.

Captain William Renton had built some sort of a sawmill here, that laid the foundation to his great fortune accumulated later at Port Blakely, a few miles to the west, to which point, he later removed. Terry afterwards gave up the contest, and removed to Seattle.

We soon pushed on over to the east where the steam from a saw-mill served as the guiding star, and landed at a point that cannot have been far removed from the western limit of the present Pioneer Place of Seattle, near where the totem pole now stands.

Here we found the never to be forgotten Yesler, not whittling his pine stick as in later years, but as a wide awake, business man, on the alert to drive a trade when an opportunity offered, or spin a yarn, if perchance time would admit. I cannot recall meeting Mr. Denny, though I made his acquaintance soon after at my own

YESLER'S FAMOUS COOK HOUSE, SEATTLE, 1853.

"I HAVE A FISH STORY OF MY OWN TO TELL"

cabin on McNeil's Island. In fact, we did not stay very long in Seattle, not being very favorably impressed with the place. There was not much of a town, probably twenty cabins in all, with a few newer frame houses. The standing timber could scarcely have been farther removed than to be out of reach of the mill, and of course, scarcely the semblance of a street. The lagoon presented an uninviting appearance and scent, where the process of filling with slabs and saw dust had already begun. The mill, though, infused activity in its immediate vicinity, and was really the life of the place.

As we were not looking for a millsite or a townsite, we pushed on north the next day. We had gone but a few miles until a favorable breeze sprang up, bringing with it visions of a happy time sailing, but with the long stretch of open waters back of us of ten miles, or more, and of several miles in width, and with no visible shelter ahead of us, or lessening of width of waters, we soon felt the breeze was not so welcome after all. We became doubtful as to the safety of sailing, and were by this time aware of the difficulty of rowing a small, flat bottom boat in rough waters with one oar sometimes in the water and the other in the air, to be suddenly reversed. While the wind was in our favor, yet the boat became almost unmanageable with the oars. The sail once down was not so easy to get up again, with the boat tipping first one way and then another, as she fell off in the trough of the waves. But finally, the sail was set again, and we scudded before the wind at a rapid rate, not feeling sure of our bearings, or what was going to happen. The bay looked to us as if it might be five miles or more wide, and in fact, with the lowering weather, we could not determine the extent. The east shore lay off to our right a half a mile or so distant, where we could see the miniature waves break on the beach, and at times, catch the sound as they rolled up on the gravel banks. We soon realized our danger, but feared to attempt a landing in the surf. Evidently the wind was increasing, the clouds were coming down lower and rain began to fall. There was but one thing to do. We must make a landing, and so the sail was hastily taken down again, and the junior of the party took to the oars, while the senior sat in the stern with paddle in hand to keep the boat steady on her course, and help a little as opportunity offered. But fortune favored us in luckily finding a smooth pebbly beach, and while we got a good drenching in landing, and the boat partially filled before we could haul her up out of reach of the surf, yet we lost nothing outright, and suffered but slight loss by damage from water. We were glad enough to go ashore and thankful that the mishap was no worse. Luckily our matches were dry and a half hour or so sufficed to build a rousing camp fire, haul our boat above high tide, and utilize it as a wind break and roof turned bottom up at an angle of forty-five degrees. Just how long we were compelled to remain in this camp, I cannot recall, but certainly two days, and I think three, but we did not explore the adjacent land much, as the rain kept us close in camp. And it was a dismal camp, although we had plenty to eat and could keep dry and warm. We here practiced the lesson taught us the evening of our first camp, by the native matron, and had plenty of clams to supplement our other provisions during the whole period, and by the time we broke up camp, concluded we were expert clam-bakers. But all such incidents must have an end, and so the time came when we broke camp and pulled for the head of Whidby's Island, a few miles off to the northwest.

And now, I have a fish story to tell. I have always been shy of telling it, lest some smart one should up and say I was just telling a yarn and drawing on my imagination, but "honor bright," I am not. But to be sure of credence, I will print the following telegram recently received, which, as it is printed in a newspaper, must be true.

Nanaimo, B. C., Friday, Jan. 29.—Another tremendous destruction of herring occurred on the shores of Protection Island a day or two ago in exactly the same way as took place near Departure Bay about three weeks ago, and to-day the entire atmosphere of the city carries the nauseous smell of thousands upon thousands of tons of decaying fish which threatens an epidemic of sickness.

The dead fish now cover the shores of Protection Island continuously for three miles to a depth ranging all the way from fifteen inches to three feet. The air is black with sea gulls. So thick have the fish been at times that were a fishing boat caught in the channel while a shoal of herring was passing, the rush of fish would literally lift the boat out of the water.

We had not proceeded far before we heard a dull sound like that often heard from the tide-rips where the current meets and disturbs the waters as like in a boiling caldron. But as we approached the disturbance, we found it was different from anything we had seen or heard before. As we rested on our oars, we could see that the disturbance was moving up toward us, and that it extended as far as we could see in the direction we were going. The sound had increased and became as like the roar of a heavy rainfall, or hailstorm in water, and we became aware that it was a vast school of fish moving south while millions were seemingly dancing on the surface of the water and leaping in the air. We could sensibly feel them striking against the boat in such vast numbers as to fairly move it as we lay at ease. The leap in the air was so high as to suggest tipping the boat to catch some as they fell back, and sure enough, here and there one would leap into the boat. We soon discovered some Indians following the school, who quickly loaded their canoes by using the barbed pole as a paddle and throwing the impaled fish into their canoes in surprising numbers. We soon obtained all we wanted by an improvised net.

We were headed for Whidby's Island, where, it was reported, rich prairie land could be found. The bay here at the head of the island was six or seven miles wide and there was no way by which we could keep near shore. Remembering the experience of a few days before, in waters not so large as here, the younger of the two confided his fears to his older companion, and that it was unwise to loiter and fish, howsoever novel and interesting, and so began pulling vigorously at the oars to find himself greatly embarassed by the mass of fish moving in the water. So far as we could see there was no end to the school ahead of us, the water, as far as the eye could reach, presenting the appearance shown with a heavy fall of hail. It did seem at times, as if the air was literally filled with fish, but we finally got rid of the moving mass, and reached the island shore in safety, only to become again weather bound in an uninhabited district of country that showed no signs of the handiwork of civilized man.

CHAPTER VIII.

Cruise on Puget Sound—Continued.

This camp did not prove so dreary as the last one, though more exposed to the swell of the big waters to the north, and sweep of the wind. To the north we had a view of thirty miles or more, where the horizon and water blend, leaving one in doubt whether land was in sight or not, though as we afterwards ascertained, our vision could reach the famous San Juan Island, later the bone of contention between our government and Great Britain. Port Townsend lay some ten miles northerly from our camp, but was shut out from view by an intervening headland. Marrowstone Point lay about midway between the two, but we did not know the exact location of the town, or for that matter, of our own. We knew, like the lost hunters, where *we* were, but the trouble was, we "didn't know where any place else was;" not lost ourselves, but the world was lost from us. In front of us, the channel of Admiralty Inlet, here, but about four miles wide, stretched out to the north into a fathomless sea of waters that for aught we knew, opened into the wide ocean. Three ships passed us while at this camp, one, coming as it would seem from out of space, a mere speck, to a full fledged, deep sea vessel, with all sails set, scudding before the wind and passing up the channel past us on the way to the anchorage of the seven vessels, the other two gracefully beating their way out against the stiff breeze to the open waters beyond. What prettier sight can one see than a full rigged vessel with all sails spread, either beating or sailing before the wind? Our enthusiam, at the sight, knew no bounds; we felt like cheering, clapping our hands, or adopting any other method of manifesting our pleasure. We had, as a matter of prudence, canvassed the question of returning from this camp as soon as released from this stress of weather, to the bay of the anchored ships in the more southern waters, but the sight of these ships, and the sight of this expanse of waters, coupled with perhaps a spirit of adventure, prompted us to quietly bide our time and to go farther, when released.

When I look back upon that decision, and in fact, upon this whole incident of my life, I stand amazed to think of the rashness of our actions and of the danger encountered from which we escaped. Not but two men with proper appliances, and with ripe experience, might with perfect security, make just such a trip, but we were possessed of neither and ran the great risks accordingly.

It was a calm, beautiful day when we reached Port Townsend, after a three hours run from our camp on the island. As we rounded Marrowstone Point, near four miles distant, the new village came into view. A feeling of surprise came over us from the supposed magnitude of the new town. Distance lends enchantment, the old adage says, but in this case the nearer we approached the embryo city, the greater our admiration. The beautiful, pebbly beach in front, the clear, level spot adjoining, with the beautiful open and comparatively level plateau in the background, and with two or three vessels at anchor in the foreground, there seemed nothing lacking to complete the picture of a perfect city site. The contrast was so great between the ill-smelling lagoon of Seattle or the dismal extensive tide flats of Olympia, that our spirits rose almost to a feeling of exultation, as the nose of our little craft grounded gently on the beach. Poor, innocent souls, we could not see beyond to discover that cities are not built upon pleasure grounds, and that there are causes beyond the ken of

man to fathom the future destiny of the embryo towns
of a new commonwealth.

We found here the enthusiastic Plummer, the plod-
ding Pettygrove and the industrious, enterprising Hast-
ings, jointly intent upon building up a town, "the greatest shipping port on the coast," as they were nearest
possible to the sea, while our Olympia friends had used
exactly the opposite arguments favoring their locality,
as "we are the farthest possible inland, where ships can
come." Small wonder that land-lubbers as we were
should become confused.

Another confusing element that pressed upon our
minds, was the vastness of the waters explored, and that
we now came to know were yet left unexplored. Then
Puget Sound was looked upon as anchorage ground from
the Straits on the north to Budd's Inlet on the south, forgetting, or rather not knowing, of the extreme depth
of waters in many places. Then that wonderful stretch
of shore line of sixteen hundred miles, with its forty or
more islands of from a few acres in extent to thirty miles
of length, with the aggregate area of waters of several
hundred square miles, exclusive of the Straits of Fuca
and Gulf of Georgia. All these marvels gradually
dawned upon our minds as we looked and counselled,
forgetting for the time the imminent risks we were taking.

Upon closer examination of the little town, we found
our first impression from the distance illusory. Many
shacks and camps, at first mistaken for the white men's
houses, were found to be occupied by the natives, a
drunken, rascally rabble, spending their gains from
the sale of fish and oil, in a debauch that would last as
long as their money was in hand.

This seemed to be a more stalwart race of Indians,
stronger and more athletic, though strictly of the class
known as fish Indians, but better developed than those
to the south, from the buffeting received in the larger

waters of the Straits, and even out in the open sea in their fishing excursions with canoes, manned by thirty or more men.

The next incident of the trip that I can remember, is when we were pulling for dear life to make a landing in front of Colonel Ebey's cabin, on Whidby's Island, opposite Port Townsend. We were carried by the rapid current quite a way past the landing, in spite of our utmost efforts. It would be a serious thing to be unable to land, as we were now in the open waters, with a fifteen mile stretch of the Straits of Fuca before us. I can remember a warm greeting at the hands of Ebey, the first time I had ever seen him. He had a droll stoppage in his speech that at first acquaintance would incline one to mirth, but after a few moments conversation, such a feeling would disappear. Of all the men we had met on the whole trip, Colonel Ebey made the most lasting impression. Somehow, what he did say came with such evident sincerity and sympathy, and with such an unaffected manner, that we were drawn close to him at once. It was while living in these same cabins where we visited him, that four years later the northern Indians, from British Columbia, came and murdered him and carried off his head as a trophy of their savage warfare.

We spent two or three days in exploring the island, only to find all the prairie land occupied, but I will not undertake from memory to name the settlers we found there. From after acquaintance, and from published reports, I came to know all of them, but do not now recall a single individual adult alive who was there then; a striking illustration of having outlived the most of my generation.

Somehow, our minds went back to the seven ships we had seen at anchor in front of Steilacoom; to the sound of the timber camps; to the bustle and stir of the

little, new village; to the greater activities that we saw
there than anywhere else on the waters of the Sound,
and likewise my thoughts would go beyond to the little
cabin on the Columbia River, and the little wife domi-
ciled there, and the other little personage, and so when
we bade Colonel Ebey good bye, it was the signal to
make our way as speedily as possible to the waters of the
seven ships.

Three days sufficed to land us back in the coveted bay
with no greater mishap than getting off our course into
the mouth of Hood's Canal, and being lost another half
day, but luckily going on the right course, the while.

But, lo and behold, the ships were gone. Not a sailing craft of any kind was in sight of the little town,
but the building activity continued. The memory of
those ships, however, remained and determined our
minds as to the important question where the trade
center was to be, and that we would look farther for the
coveted spot upon which to make a home.

I look back with amazement at the rash undertaking
of that trip, so illy provided, and inexperienced, as we
were, and wonder that we escaped with no more serious
mishap than we had. We were not justified in taking
these chances, or at least I was not, with the two depen-
dents left in the cabin on the bank of the Columbia
River, but we did not realize the danger until we were
in it, and hence did not share in the suspense, and uneasiness of that one left behind. Upon the whole, it was
a most enjoyable trip, and one, barring the risk and
physical inability to play my part, I could with great
enjoyment encounter the same adventure of which I have
only related a mere outline. Did you ever, reader, take
a drive, we will say in a hired outfit, with a paid coach-
man, and then take the lines in your own hands by way
of contrast? If so, then you will realize the thrill of
enjoyment where you pull your own oars, sail your own

craft, cook your own dinner, and lie in your own bed of boughs, and go when and where you will with that keen relish incident to the independence and uncertainties of such a trip. It was a wild, reckless act, but we came out stronger than ever in the faith of the great future in store for the north country, where we finally made our home and where I have lived ever since, now over fifty years.

CHAPTER IX.

From Columbia River to Puget Sound.

"Can I get home to-night?" I asked myself, while the sun was yet high one afternoon of the last week of June (1853).

I was well up river, on the left bank of the Cowlitz. I could not tell how far, for there were no mile stones, or way places to break the monotony of the crooked, half obstructed trail leading down stream. I knew that at the best it would be a race with the sun, for there were many miles between me and the cabin, but the days were long, and the twilight longer, and I would camp that much nearer home if I made haste. My pack had been discarded on the Sound; I did not even have either coat or blanket. The heavy, woolen shirt, often worn outside the pants, will be well remembered by my old time pioneer readers. Added to this, the well worn slouch hat, and worn shoes, both of which gave ample ventilation, completed my dress; socks, I had none, neither suspenders; the improvised belt taking their place, and so I was dressed suitable for the race, and was eager for the trial.

I had parted with my brother at Olympia, where he had come to set me that far on my journey; he to return to the claims we had taken, and I to make my way across country for the wife and baby, to remove them to our new home. I did not particularly mind the camping so much if necessary, but did not fancy the idea of lying out so near home, if I could by extra exertion reach the cabin that night. I did not have the friendly ox to snug up to for warmth, as in so many bivouacs,

while on the plains, but I had matches, and there were
many mossy places for a bed and friendly shelter of the
drooping cedars. We never thought of "catching cold,"
by lying on the ground or on cedar boughs, or from
getting a good drenching. Somehow it did seem I was
free from all care of bodily ailment, and could endure
continued exertion for long hours without the least inconvenience. The readers of this generation doubtless
will be ready to pour out their sympathy for the hardships of the lone trail, and lone camp, and the supperless
bed of boughs, but they may as well reserve this for
others of the pioneers whose systems were less able to
bear the unusual strain of the new conditions. But the
camp had to be made; the cabin could not be reached,
for the trail could not be followed at night, nor the
Kalama Creek crossed; so, slackening my pace at nightfall to gradually cool my system, I finally made my camp
and slept as sound as if on a bed of down, with the consolation that the night was short and that I could see
to travel by 3 o'clock, and it did not make so very much
difference, after all.

I can truly say that of all those years of camp and
cabin life, I do not look upon them as years of hardship.
To be sure, our food was plain as well as dress, our hours
of labor long and labor frequently severe, and that the
pioneers appeared rough and uncouth, yet underlying
all this, there ran a vein of good cheer, of hopefulness,
of the intense interest always engendered with strife to
overcome difficulties where one is the employer as well
as the employed. We never watched for the sun to go
down, or for the seven o'clock whistle, or for the boss to
quicken our steps, for the days were always too short,
and interest in our work always unabated.

The cabin could not be seen for a long distance on the
trail, but I thought I caught sight of a curl of smoke
and then immediately knew I did, and that settled it
that all was well in the cabin. But when a little nearer,

a little lady in almost bloomer dress was espied milking a cow, and a frisking, fat calf in the pen was seen,
then I knew, and all solicitude vanished. The little
lady never finished milking that cow, nor did she
ever milk others when the husband was at home, though
she knew how well enough, and never felt above such
work if a necessity arose, but we parceled out duties on
a different basis, with each to their suited parts. The
bloom on the cheek of the little wife, the baby in the
cabin as fat as the calf, told the story of good health
and plenitude of food, and brought good cheer with the
welcome home. The dried potato eyes had just been
planted, although it was then the first week of July, following the receding waters of the June freshet up the
Columbia, and were sprouting vigorously. I may say,
in passing, there came a crop from these of nearly four
hundred bushels at harvest time.

It did seem there were so many things to talk about
that one could scarcely tell where to begin or when to
stop. Why, at Olympia, eggs were a dollar a dozen. I
saw them selling at that. That butter you have there
on the shelf would bring a dollar a pound as fast as
you could weigh it out; I saw stuff they called butter
sell for that; then potatoes were selling for $3.00 a
bushel and onions at $4.00. Everything the farmer
raises sells high. "Who buys?" "Oh, almost everbody
has to buy; there's the ships and the timber camps, and
the hotels, and the—

"Where do they get the money?"

"Why, everybody seems to have money. Some take it
there with them. Then men working in the timber
camps get $4.00 a day and their board. I saw one place
where they paid $4.00 a cord for wood to ship to San
Francisco, and one can sell all the shingles he can make
at $4.00 a thousand, and I was offered 5 cents a foot for
piles. If we had Buck and Dandy over there we could
make twenty dollars a day putting in piles."

"Where could you get the piles?"

"Off the government land, of course. All help themselves to all they want. Then there are the fish, and the clams, and the oysters, and—"

"But, what about the land for a claim?"

That question was a stumper. The little wife never lost sight of that bargain made before we were married, that we were going to be farmers; and here now I found myself praising a country I could not say much for its agricultural qualities, but other things quite foreign to that interest.

But if we could sell produce higher, might we not well lower our standard of an ideal farm? The claim I had taken was described with a tinge of disappointment, falling so far below in quality of what we had hoped to acquire, and still adhering to the resolution to be farmers, we began the preparations for removal to the Sound.

The wife, baby, bedding, ox yoke, and log chain, were sent up the Cowlitz in a canoe, while Buck and Dandy and I renewed our acquaintance by taking to the trail where we had our parting bivouac. We had camped together many a night on the plains, and slept together literally, not figuratively. I used to crowd up close under Buck's back while napping on watch, for the double purpose of warmth and signal—warmth while at rest, signal if the ox moved. On this occasion I was illy prepared for a cool night camp, having neither blanket, nor coat, as I had expected to reach "Hard-Bread's" Hotel, where the people in the canoe would stop over night. But I could not make it and so again laid on the trail to renew the journey bright and early the next morning.

Hard Bread's is an odd name for a hotel, you will say; so it is, but the name grew out of the fact that Gardner, the old widower that kept "bachelor's" hall at the mouth of Toutle River (opposite Pumphrey's place, on the left bank of the Cowlitz), fed his cus-

tomers on hard tack three times a day, if perchance
any one was unfortunate enough to be compelled to take
three meals at his place.

I found the little wife had not fared any better than
I had on the trail, and in fact, not so well, for the floor
of the cabin was a good deal harder than the sand spit
where I had passed the night, with plenty of pure, fresh
air, while she, in a closed cabin, in the same room with
many others, could neither boast of fresh air, nor freedom from creeping things that make life miserable.
With her shoes for a pillow, a shawl for covering, small
wonder the report came "I did not sleep a wink, last
night."

Judge Olney and wife were passengers in the same
canoe and guests at the same house with the wife, as
also Frank Clark, who afterwards played a prominent
part at the bar, and in the political affairs of Pierce
County in particular, and incidentally of the whole Territory.

We soon arrived at the Cowlitz landing, and at the
end of the canoe journey, so, striking the tent that had
served us so well on the plains, and with a cheerful camp
fire blazing for cooking, speedily forgot the experience
of the trail, the cramped passage in the canoe, the hard
bread, dirt and all, while enjoying the savory meal, the
like of which only the expert hands of the ladies of the
plains could prepare.

But now we had fifty miles of land to travel before
us, and over *such* a road! Words cannot describe that
road, and so I will not try. One must have traveled it
to fully comprehend what it meant. However, we had
one consolation, and that was it would be worse in
winter than at that time. We had no wagon. Our
wagon had been left at the Dalles, and we never saw
nor heard of it again. Our cows were gone—given for
provender to save the lives of the oxen during the deep
December snow, and so when we took account of stock,

we had Buck and Dandy, the baby, and a tent, an ox yoke and chain, enough clothing and bedding to keep us comfortable, with but very little food and no money— that had all been expended on the canoe passage.

Shall we pack the oxen and walk, and carry baby, or shall we build a sled and drag our things over to the Sound, or shall I make an effort to get a wagon? This latter proposition was the most attractive, and so next morning, driving Buck and Dandy before me, leaving the wife and baby to take care of the camp, the search for a wagon began.

That great hearted, old pioneer, John R. Jackson, did not hesitate a moment, stranger as I was, to say "Yes, you can have two if you need them." Jackson had settled eight years before, ten miles out from the landing, and had an abundance around him, and like all those earlier pioneers, took a pride in helping others who came later. Retracing the road, night found me again in camp, and all hands happy, but Jackson would not listen to allowing us to proceed the next day any farther than his premises, where he would entertain us in his comfortable cabin, and send us on our way the morning following, rejoicing in plenty.

Without special incident or accident, we in due time arrived at the foot of the falls of the Deschutes (Tumwater), and on the shore of Puget Sound. Here camp must be established again; the little wife and baby left while I drove the wagon over the tedious road to Jackson's and then returned with the oxen to tide water.

The reader may well imagine my feelings, when, upon my return, my tent, wife, baby, and all were gone. We knew before I started on my return trip that smallpox was raging among the Indians, and that a camp where this disease was prevalent was in sight less than a quarter of a mile away. The present day reader must remember that dread disease had terrors then that, since universal vaccination, it does not now possess. Could it be possible my folks had been taken sick and had been removed? The question, however, was soon solved. I had scarcely gotten out of sight upon my trip before one of those royal pioneer matrons came to the camp and pleaded and insisted and finally almost frightened the little wife to go and share her house with her which was near by, and be out of danger from the smallpox.

And that was the way we traveled from the Columbia River to Puget Sound.

God bless those earlier pioneers; they were all good to us, sometimes to the point of embarassment by their generous hospitality.

I cannot dismiss this subject without reverting to one such, in particular, who gave his whole crop during this winter of which I have just written, to start immigrants on the road to prosperity, and in some instances, to prevent suffering.

In consequence of the large immigration and increased demand, prices of provisions had run sky high, and out of reach of some of the recent immigrants with large families. George Bush had squatted on a claim seven miles south of Olympia, in 1845, and had an abundance of farm produce, but would not sell a pound of anything to a speculator; but to immigrants, for seed or for immediate, pressing wants, to all alike, without money and without price—"return it when you can,"— he would say, and so divided up his whole crop, then worth thousands of dollars. And yet this man's oath could not at that time be taken; neither could he sue in the courts or acquire title to the land upon which he lived, or any land. He had negro blood in his veins, and under the law of this great country, then, was a proscribed outcast. Conditions do change as time passes. The wrong was so flagrant in this particular case that a special act of Congress enabled this old, big-hearted pioneer of 1845 to hold his claim, and his descendents are living on it yet.

CHAPTER X.

The Second Cabin.

What I am now about to write may provoke a smile, but I can only say, reader, put yourself in my place. That there should be a feeling akin to affection between a man and an ox will seem past comprehension to many. The time had come that Buck and Dandy and I must part for good and all. I could not transport them to our island home, neither provide for them. These patient, dumb brutes had been my close companions for the long, weary months on the plains, and had never failed me; they would do my bidding to the letter. I often said Buck understood English better than some people I had seen in my life time. I had done what not one in a hundred did; that was, to start on that trip with an unbroken ox and cow team. I had selected these four-year-old steers for their intelligent eyes as well as for their trim build, and had made no mistake. We had bivouacked together; actually slept together, lunched together. They knew me as far as they could see, and seemed delighted to obey my word, and I did regret to feel constrained to part with them. I knew they had assured my safe transit on the weary journey, if not even to the point of having saved my life. I could pack them, ride them, drive them by the word and receive their salutations, and why should I be ashamed to part with feelings of more than regret.

But I had scant time to spend on sentiment. The brother did not expect my return so soon. The island claim, (and cabin, as I thought) must be reached; the little skiff obtained in which to transport the wife and baby, not yet feeling willing to trust them in a canoe.

So, without further ado, a small canoe was chartered, and my first experience to "paddle my own canoe" materialized. It seemed this same place where we had our first clam bake was the sticking point again. The tide turned, night overtook me, and I could go no farther. Two men were in a cabin, the Doctor Johnson, heretofore mentioned and a man by the name of Hathaway, both drunk and drinking, with a jug handy by, far from empty. Both were men that seemed to me to be well educated, and, if sober, refined. They quoted from Burns, sang songs and ditties, laughed and danced until late in the night, when they became exhausted and fell asleep. They would not listen to my suggestion that I would camp and sleep outside the cabin, and I could not sleep inside, so the night passed off without rest or sleep until the tide turned, and I was glad enough to slip away, leaving them in their stupor.

A few miles vigorous paddling brought me to McNeil Island, opposite the town of Steilacoom, where I expected to find our second cabin, my brother and the boat. No cabin, no brother, no boat, were to be seen. A raft of cabin logs floating in the lagoon near by, where the United States penitentiary now stands, was all the signs to be seen, other than what was there when I left the place for my return trip to the Columbia River. I was sorely puzzled as to what to do. My brother was to have had the cabin ready by the time I returned. He not only had not done that, but had taken the boat, and left no sign as to where it or he could be found. Not knowing what else to do I mechanically paddled over to the town, where, sure enough, the boat was anchored, but nobody knew where the man had gone. I finally found where the provisions had been left, and, after an earnest parley, succeeded in getting possession. I took my canoe in tow and soon made my way back to where the little folks were, and speedily transferred the whole outfit to the spot that was to be our island home; set up our tent, and felt at home once more.

The village, three miles away, across the bay, had grown during my absence and in the distance looked like a city in fact as well as in name. The mountain looked bigger and taller than ever. Even the songs of the Indians sounded better, and the canoes seemed more graceful, and the paddles wielded more expertly. Everything looked cheerful, even to the spouting clams on the beach, and the crow's antics of breaking clams by rising in the air and dropping them on the boulders. So many new things to show the folks that I for a time almost forgot we were about out of provisions and money, and did not know what had happened to the brother. Thoughts of these suddenly coming upon us, our spirits fell, and for a time we could hardly say we were perfectly happy.

"I believe that canoe is coming straight here," said the little wife, the next morning, about nine o'clock. All else is dropped, and a watch set upon the strange craft, moving slowly, apparently in the long distance, but more rapidly as it approached, and there sat the brother. Having returned to the village and finding that the boat and provisions had been taken, and seeing smoke in the bight, he knew what had happened, and, following his own good impulse, we were soon together again, and supremely happy. He had received a tempting offer to help load a ship, and had just completed his contract, and was able to exhibit a "slug" * of money and more besides that looked precious in our eyes.

The building of the cabin with its stone fire-place, cat-and-clay chimney, its lumber floor, real window with glass in it, together with the high post bedstead out of tapering cedar saplings, the table fastened to the wall,

---

*A "slug" was fifty dollars value in gold, minted by private parties, in octagon form, and passed current the same as if it had borne the government's stamp. "Slugs" were worth as much melted as in the coined form. My ideas about the gold standard were formed at that time, and I may say my mind never changed on this subject.

with rustic chairs, seemed but like a play spell. No eight hour a day work there—eighteen would be nearer the mark—we never tired.

There came a letter: "Boys, if Oliver will come back to cross with us, we will go to Oregon next year," this signed by the father, then fifty years old. The letter was nearly three months old when we received it. What should we say and what should we do? Would Davenport pay for the Columbia River claims and the prospective potato crop in the fall—could he? We will say yes, Oliver will be with you next Spring. We must go to the timber camp to earn the money to pay expenses of the trip and not depend altogether on the Columbia River asset.

"What shall we do with the things?" said the little wife.

"Lock them up in the cabin," said the elder brother.

"And you go and stay with Dofflemire," said the young husband.

"Not I," said the little wife, "I'm going along to cook," and thus it was that all our well laid plans were suddenly changed, our clearing land deferred, the chicken house, the inmates of which were to make us rich, was not to be built, the pigs were not brought to fatten on the clams, and many other pet schemes dropped that we might accomplish this one object, that Oliver might go back to Iowa to "bring the father out" across the plains.

We struck rapid, heavy, but awkward strokes in the timber camp established on the bluff overlooking the falls at Tumwater, while the little wife supplied the huckleberry pudding for dinner, plenty of the lightest, whitest bread, vegetables, meat, and fish served in style good enough for kings; such appetites! No coaxing required to eat a hearty meal; such sound sleep; such satisfaction! Talk about your hardships. We would have none of it. It was a pleasure as we counted the

"WE STRUCK RAPID, HEAVY, BUT AWKWARD STROKES."

eleven dollars a day that the Tullis brothers paid us for cutting logs, at one dollar and seventy cents a thousand, which we earned every day, and Sundays, too, seventy-seven dollars a week. Yes, we were going to make it. "Make what?" the reader will say. Why succeed in getting enough money together to pay the passage of the elder brother to Iowa. And what a trip. Over to the Columbia River, out from there by steamer to San Francisco, then to the Isthmus, then New York after which by rail as far west as there was a railroad and then walk to Eddyville, Iowa, from where the start was again to be made.

Again the younger brother was left without money and but a scant supply of provisions, and winter had come on. The elder brother was speeding on his way, and could not be heard from frequently. How our little family succeeded in getting enough together to eat is not an interesting topic for the general reader. Suffice to say, we always secured abundance, even if at times the variety was restricted.

It was soon after Oliver's departure that I first made the acquaintance of Dr. Tolmie. It was upon the occasion when our new baby was born, now the mother of eight grown up children, and several times a grandmother, Mrs. Ella Templeton of Halsey, Oregon.

Of course, Dr. Tolmie did not practice medicine. He had the cares of the great foreign corporation, the Puget Sound Agricultural Company, on his shoulders. He was harassed by the settlers, who chafed because a foreign corporation had fenced up quite large tracts of grazing and some farming lands, and had thousands of sheep and cattle on the range. Constant friction was the result. The cattle were wild; therefore, some settler would kill one every now and then, and make the remainder still wilder, and again, therefore, the more the reason that others might be killed. The Doctor was a patient, tactful man, with an impulse to always do one a good turn for the sake of doing it. Consequently, when asked to attend, he did so without hesitation, though the request came from a perfect stranger and compliance was to his great inconvenience, yet without fee and without expectation of ever meeting the parties again. This first acquaintance ripened into friendship life long, that became closer as he neared his end. But recently, fifty years after this event, I have had the pleasure of a visit from two of his daughters, and I may say there has been scarcely a year in all this time but some token of friendship has passed. He was a noble man, with noble impulses. He died on his farm near Victoria many years ago.

Soon after this, I made my first acquaintance with Arthur A. Denny. It came about this way. He and two other gentlemen were returning from the first Territorial Legislature, then just adjourned. Wind and tide compelled them to suspend their journey from Olympia to Seattle, and to stay over night with us in the little cabin. This was early in May, 1854. Mr. Denny remarked in the morning that he thought there was a good foundation under my cabin floor, as he did not find any spring to the bed. He and his companion laid on the floor, but I remember we did not go to bed very early. All during the session we had heard a great deal about removing the capital of the Territory from Olympia to Steilacoom. The legislature had adjourned and no action had been taken, and, in fact, no bill for the purpose was introduced. Mr. Denny said that before the recess a clear majority of both houses were in favor of removal to Steilacoom, but for the mistake of Lafayette Balch, member of the council from Pierce County, the removal would have been accomplished. Balch, so Denny told me, felt so sure of his game that he did not press to a vote before the recess.

At that, the first session of the Legislature, the mania was for Territorial roads; everybody wanted a Territorial road. One, projected from Seattle to Bellingham Bay, did not meet with approval by Balch. Stroking his long beard as he was wont to do almost mechanically, he "thought they had gone far enough in establishing roads for one session." It was impolitic in the highest degree for Balch to offend the northern members in this way, as also unnecessary, as usually these roads remained on paper only, and cost nothing. However, he lost his majority in the council, and so the project died, to the very great disappointment of the people of Steilacoom and surrounding country.

CHAPTER XI.

Trip Through the Natchess Pass.

The latter part of August, 1854, James K. Hurd, of Olympia, sent me word that he had been out on the immigrant trail and heard that some of my relations on the road were belated and short of provisions. He advised that I should go to their assistance, and particularly if I wanted to be sure they should come direct to Puget Sound over the Cascade Mountains, and not go down the Columbia River into Oregon. How it could be, with the experience of my brother Oliver to guide them, that my people should be in the condition described, was past my comprehension. However, I accepted the statement as true and particularly felt the importance of their having certain knowledge as to prevailing conditions of an over-mountain trip through the Natchess Pass. But how could I go and leave wife and two babies on our island home? The summer had been spent clearing land and planting crops, and my finances were very low. To remove my family would cost money, besides the abandonment of the season's work to almost certain destruction. The wife said at once, and without a moment's hesitation, to go, and she and Mrs. Darrow, who was with us as nurse and companion friend, would stay "right where we are until you get back," with a confidence in which I did not share. The trip at best was hazardous to an extent, even when undertaken well prepared and with company. So far as I could see, I might have to go on foot and pack my food and blanket on my back, and I knew that I would have to go alone. I knew some work had

been done on the road during the summer, but was
unable to get definite information as to whether any
camps were yet left in the mountains, and did not have
that abiding faith in my ability to get back that rested
in the breast of the little, courageous wife, but I dared
not impart my forebodings to harass and intensify her
fears and disturb her peace of mind while absent. The
immigration the previous year, as related elsewhere,
had encountered formidable difficulties in the mountains, narrowly escaping the loss of everything if not
facing actual starvation. Reports were current that
the government appropriation for a military road had
been expended, and that the road was passable for teams,
but a like report had been freely circulated the previous
year, with results almost disastrous to those attempting
to come through. I could not help feeling that possibly
the same conditions yet existed. The only way to determine the question was to go and see for myself; meet
my father's party and pilot them through the pass.

It was on the third day of September of 1854 that I
left home. I had been planting turnips for two days,
and made a memorandum of the date, and by that fix
the date of my departure. Of that turnip crop I shall
have more to say later, as it had a cheering effect upon
the incoming immigrants.

At Steilacoom there was a character then understood
by few, and I may say by not many even to the end, in
whom somehow, I had implicit confidence. Dr. J. B.
Webber, afterwards of the firm of Balch & Webber, of
Steilacoom, the largest shipping and mercantile firm on
the Sound, was a very eccentric man. Between him and
myself, there would seem to be a gulf that could not be
closed. Our habits of life were as diametrically opposite as possible for two men to be. He was always drinking; never sober, neither ever drunk. I would never
touch a drop while the doctor would certainly drink a
dozen times a day, just a little at a time, but seemingly

tippling all the time.   Then, he openly kept an Indian
woman in defiance of the sentiment of all the families
of the community.   He was addicted to other vices
which I will not here relate.   It was with this man that
I entrusted the safe keeping of my little family.   I
knew my wife had such an aversion to this class that I
did not even tell her with whom I would arrange to look
out for her welfare, but suggested another to whom she
might apply in case of need.   I knew Dr. Webber for
long years afterwards, and until the day of his horrible
death with delirium tremens, and never had my faith
shaken as to the innate goodness of the man.   Why
these contrary traits of character should be, I cannot
say, but so it was.   His word was as good as his bond,
and his impulses were all directly opposite to his personal habits.   Twice a week an Indian woman visited
the cabin on the island, always with some little presents
and making inquiries about the babies and whether there
was anything needed, with the parting *"alki nika keel-
apie"* (by and by I will return) ; and she did, every few
days during my absence.

When I spoke to Webber about what I wanted, he
seemed pleased to be able to do a kind act, and, to reas-
sure me, got out his field glass and turned it on the
cabin across the water, three miles distant.   Looking
through it intently for a moment and handing the glass
to me, said, "I can see everything going on over there,
and you need have no uneasiness about your folks while
gone," and I did not.

With a fifty pound flour sack filled with hard bread,
or navy biscuit, a small piece of dried venison, a couple
of pounds of cheese, a tin cup and half of a three point
blanket, all made into a pack of less than forty pounds,
I climbed the hill at Steilacoom and took the road leading to Puyallup, and spent the night with Jonathan Mc-
Carty, near where the town of Sumner now is.

McCarty said "you can't get across the streams on foot; I will let you have a pony. He is small, but sure-footed, and hardy, and will in any event carry you across the rivers." McCarty also said: "Tell your folks this is the greatest grass country on earth; why, I am sure I harvested five tons of timothy to the acre this year." Upon my expressing a doubt, he said he knew he was correct by the measurement of the mow in the barn and the land. In after years, I came to know he was correct, though at the time, I could not help but believe he was mistaken.

The next day found me on the road with my blanket under the saddle, my sack of hard bread strapped on behind the saddle, and myself mounted to ride on level stretches of the road, or across streams, of which, as will appear later, I had full forty crossings to make, but had only one ahead of me the first day. That one, though, as the Englishman would say, was a "nasty" one, across White River at Porter's place.

White River on the upper reaches is a roaring torrent only at all fordable in low water and in but few places. The rush of waters can be heard for a mile or more from the high bluff overlooking the narrow valley, or rather canyon, and presented a formidable barrier for a lone traveler. The river bed is full of boulders worn rounded and smooth and slippery, from the size of a man's head to very much larger, thus making footing for animals uncertain. After my first crossing, I dreaded those to come, which I knew were ahead of me, more than all else of the trip, for a misstep of the pony meant fatal results in all probability. The little fellow, though, seemed to be equal to the occasion. If the footing became too uncertain, he would stop stock still, and pound the water with one foot and finally reach out carefully until he could find secure footing, and then move up a step or two. The water of the river is so charged with the sediment from the glaciers above, that the bottom

could not be seen—only felt—hence the absolute necessity of feeling one's way. It is wonderful, the sagacity or instinct or intelligence, or whatever we may call
it, manifested by the horse. I immediately learned that
my pony could be trusted on the fords better than myself, thereafter I held only a supporting, but not a guiding rein, and he carried me safely over the forty crossings on my way out, and my brother as many on the
return trip.

Allen Porter then lived near the first crossing, on the
farther side, and as this was the last settler I would see
and the last place I could get feed for my pony, other
than grass or browse, I put up for the night under his
roof. He said I was going on a "Tom fool's errand," for
my folks could take care of themselves, and tried to
dissuade me from proceeding on my journey. But I
would not be turned back, and the following morning
cut loose from the settlements and, figuratively speaking, plunged into the deep forest of the mountains.

The road (if it could be properly called a road), lay
in the narrow valley of White River, or on the mountains adjacent, in some places (as at Mud Mountain),
reaching an altitude of more than a thousand feet above
the river bed. Some places the forest was so dense
that one could scarcely see to read at mid-day, while
in other places large burns gave an opening for day-
light.

During the forenoon of this first day, while in one of
those deepest of deep forests, where, if the sky was clear,
and one could catch a spot you could see out overhead,
one might see the stars as from a deep well, my pony
stopped short, raised his head with his ears pricked up,
indicating something unusual was at hand. Just then,
I caught an indistinct sight of a movement ahead, and
thought I heard voices, while the pony made an effort
to turn and flee in the opposite direction. Soon there
appeared three women and eight children on foot, com-

ing down the road in blissful ignorance of the presence
of any one but themselves in the forest.

"Why, stranger! Where on earth did you come from?
Where are you going to, and what are you here for?"
was asked by the foremost woman of the party, in such
quick succession as to utterly preclude any answer, as
she discovered me standing on the road holding my un-
easy pony. Mutual explanations soon followed. I soon
learned their teams had become exhausted, and that
all the wagons but one had been left, and this one was
on the road a few miles behind them; that they were
entirely out of provisions and had had nothing to eat
for twenty hours, except what natural food they had
gathered, which was not much. They eagerly inquired
the distance to food, which I thought they might possibly reach that night, but in any event the next morning early. Meanwhile I had opened my sack of hard
bread and gave each a cracker, in the eating of which
the sound resembled pigs cracking dry, hard corn.

Of those eleven persons, I only know of but one now
alive, although, of course, the children soon outgrew my
knowledge of them, but they never forgot me.

Mrs. Anne Fawcet, the spokesman of the party, I
knew well in after years, and although now eighty years
old (she will pardon me for telling her age), is living in
good circumstances a mile out from the town of Auburn, nearly twenty miles south of Seattle, and but a
couple of miles from the scene of the dreadful massacre
related elsewhere, and also where the gallant Lieuten-
ant Slaughter lost his life.

Mrs. Fawcet can scarcely be called a typical pioneer
woman, yet there were many approaching her ways. She
was of too independent a character to be molded into that
class; too self-reliant to be altogether like her neighbor housewives; and yet was possessed of those sturdy
virtues so common with the pioneer—industry and fru-
gality, coupled with unbounded hospitality. The other

ladies of the party, Mrs. Herpsberger and Mrs. Hall, I never knew afterwards, and have no knowledge as to their fate, other than that they arrived safely in the settlements.

But we neither of us had time to parley or visit, and so the ladies with their children, barefoot and ragged, bareheaded and unkempt, started down the mountain intent on reaching food, while I started up the road wondering whether or not this scene was to be often repeated as I advanced on my journey. A dozen biscuits of hard bread is usually a very small matter, but with me it might mean a great deal. How far would I have to go? When could I find out? What would be the plight of my people when found? Or would I find them at all? Might they not pass by and be on the way down the Columbia River before I could reach the main immigrant trail? These and kindred questions weighed heavily on my mind as I slowly and gradually ascended the mountain.

Some new work on the road gave evidence that men had recently been there, but the work was so slight one could easily believe immigrants might have done it as they passed. Fifteen thousand dollars had been appropriated by Congress for a military road, which report said would be expended in improving the way cut by the immigrants and citizens through the Natchess Pass during the summer of 1853. I saw some of the work, but do not remember seeing any of the men, as I stuck close to the old trail, and so my first camp was made alone, west of the summit and without special incident. I had reached an altitude where the night chill was keenly felt, and, with my light blanket, missed the friendly contact of the back of the faithful ox that had served me so well on the plains. My pony had nothing but browse for supper, and was restless. Nevertheless I slept soundly and was up early, refreshed and ready to resume the journey.

CHAPTER XII.

Trip Through the Natchess Pass—Continued.

It is strange how the mind will vividly retain the
memory of some incidents of no particular importance
while the recollection of other passing events so completely fades away. I knew I had to cross that ugly
stream, White River, five times during the first day's
travel, but cannot recall but one crossing, where my
pony nearly lost his balance, and came down on his
knees with his nose in the water for the moment, but to
recover and bravely carry me out safely.

The lone camp well up on the mountain had chilled
me, but the prospect before me and that I had left behind brought a depressed feeling most difficult to
describe. I had passed through long stretches of forest
so tall and so dense that it seemed incredible that such
did exist anywhere on earth. And then, the road; such
a road, if it could be called a road. Curiously enough,
the heavier the standing timber, the easier it had been
to slip through with wagons, there being but little un-
decayed or down timber. In the ancient of days, however, great giants had been uprooted lifting considerable
earth with the upturned roots, that, as time went on
and the roots decayed, formed mounds two, three, or
four feet high, leaving a corresponding hollow in which
one would plunge, the whole being covered by a dense,
short, evergreen growth, completely hiding from view
the unevenness of the ground. Over these hillocks and
hollows the immigrants had rolled their wagon wheels,
and over the large roots of the fir, often as big as one's
body and nearly all of them on top of the ground. I

will not undertake to say how many of these giant
trees were to be found to the acre, but they were so
numerous and so large that in many places it was difficult to find a passage way between them, and then
only by a tortuous route winding in various directions.
When the timber burns were encountered the situation
was worse.   Often the remains of timber would be
piled in such confusion that sometimes wagons could
pass under logs that rested on others; then again, others
were encountered half buried, while still others would
rest a foot or so from the ground, these, let the reader
remember, oftentimes were five feet or more in diameter,
with trunks from two to three hundred feet in length.
All sorts of devices had been resorted to in order to
overcome these obstructions.   In many cases, where
not too large, cuts had been taken out, while in other
places, the larger timber had been bridged up to by
piling smaller logs, rotten chunks, brush, or earth, so
the wheels of the wagon could be rolled up over the
body of the tree.   Usually three notches would be cut
on the top of the log, two for the wheels and one for the
reach or coupling pole to pass through.

In such places, the oxen would be taken to the opposite side, a chain or rope run to the end of the tongue,
a man to drive, one or two to guide the tongue, others
to help at the wheels, and so with infinite labor and
great care the wagons would gradually be worked down
the mountain in the direction of the settlements.   Small
wonder that the immigrants of the previous year should
report they had to cut their way through the timber,
while the citizen road workers had reported that the
road was opened, and small wonder that the prospect
of the road should have as chilling effect on my mind
as the chill mountain air had had on my body.

But, the more difficulties encountered, the more determined I became, at all hazards, to push through, for
the more the necessity to acquaint myself with the

obstacles to be encountered and to be with my friends to encourage and help them. Before me lay the great range or pass, five thousand feet above sea level, and the rugged mountain climb to get to the summit, and the summit prairies where my pony could have a feast of grass. It was on this summit hill the immigration of the previous year had encountered such grave difficulties. At the risk of in part repeating, I am tempted to quote some of my own words to a select party of friends, the teachers of the county in which I have lived so long, prepared for that special occasion.

"About twenty miles north of the great mountain of the Cascade range is a picturesque, small scope of open country known as Summit Prairie, in the Natchess Pass, some seventy miles southeasterly from this city (Tacoma). In this prairie, fifty years ago this coming autumn, a camp of immigrants was to be seen. * * * Go back they could not; either they must go ahead or starve in the mountains. A short way out from the camp a steep mountain declivity lay square across their track. As one of the ladies of the party said, when she first saw it: 'Why, Lawsee Massee! We have come to the jumping off place at last!' This lady felt, as many others of the party felt, like they had come to the end of the world (to them), and the exclamation was not for the stage effect, but one of fervent prayer for deliverance.

"Stout hearts in the party were not to be deterred from making the effort to go ahead. Go around this hill they could not; go down it with logs trailed to the wagons, as they had done before, they could not, as the hill was so steep the logs would go end over end and be a danger instead of a help. So the rope they had was run down the hill and found to be too short to reach the bottom. One of the leaders of the party (I knew him well) turned to his men and said, 'Kill a steer;' and they killed a steer, cut his hide into strips and spliced it to the rope. It was found yet to be too short to reach to the bottom. The order went out: 'Kill two more steers!' And two more steers were killed, their hides cut into strips and spliced to the rope,

which then reached the bottom of the hill; and by the aid
of that rope and strips of the hides of those three steers,
twenty-nine wagons were lowered down the mountain side
to the bottom of the steep hill.

"Now, my friends, there is no fiction about this story,—
it is a true story, and some of the actors are yet alive, and
some of them live in this county. Nor were their trials
ended when they got their wagons down to the bottom of
that hill.

"Does it now seem possible for mortal man to do this?
And yet this is only a plain statement of an incident of pioneer life without giving any names and dates, that can yet
be verified by living witnesses; but these witnesses are
not for here long.

"James Biles, who afterwards settled near Olympia, was
the man who ordered the steers killed to procure the hides
to lengthen out the rope. Geo. H. Himes, of Portland, who
is still living, was one of the party; so was Stephen Judson,
of Steilacoom; also Nelson Sargeant, of Grand Mound, now
a very old man.

"The feat of bringing that train of twenty-nine wagons
in with the loss of only one is the greatest of anything I
ever knew or heard of in the way of pioneer travel.

"With snail-like movements, the cattle and men becoming weaker and weaker, progress was made each day
until finally it seemed as if the oxen could do no more, and
it became necessary to send them forward on the trail ten
miles, where it was known plenty of grass could be had.
Meantime the work on the road continued until the third
day, when the last particle of food was gone. The teams
were brought back, the trip over the whole ten miles made,
and Connell's Prairie reached at dark.

"The struggle over that ten miles, where to a certain extent each party became so intent on their particular surroundings as to forget all else, left the women and children
to take care of themselves while the husbands tugged at the
wagons. I now have in mind to relate the experience of
one of these mothers with a ten-year-old boy, one child of
four years and another of eight months.

"Part of the time these people traveled on the old trail and part on the newly-cut road, and by some means fell behind the wagons, which forded that turbulent, dangerous stream, White River, before they reached the bank, and were out of sight, not knowing but the women and children were ahead.

"I wish every little boy of ten years of age of this great State, or, for that matter, twenty years old or more, could read and profit by what I am now going to relate, especially if that little or big boy at times thinks he is having a hard time because he is asked to help his mother or father at odd times, or perchance to put in a good solid day's work on Saturday, instead of spending it as a holiday; or if he has a cow to milk or wood to split, or anything that is work, to make him bewail his fate for having such a hard time in life. I think the reading of the experience of this little ten-year-old boy with his mother and the two smaller children would encourage him to feel more cheerful and more content with his lot.

"As I have said, the wagons had passed on, and there these four people were on the right bank of the river while their whole company was on the opposite bank and had left them there alone.

"A large fallen tree reached across the river, but the top on the further side lay so close to the water that a constant trembling and swaying made the trip dangerous.

"None of them had eaten anything since the previous day, and but a scant supply then; but the boy resolutely shouldered the four-year-old and safely deposited him on the other side. Then came next the little tot, the baby, to be carried in arms across. Next came the mother.

" 'I can't go!' she exclaimed; 'it makes me so dizzy.'

" 'Put one hand over your eyes, mother, and take hold of me with the other,' said the boy; and so they began to move out sideways on the log, a half step at a time.

" 'Hold steady, mother; we are nearly over.'

" 'Oh, I am gone!' was the only response, as she lost her balance and fell into the river, but happily so near the farther bank that the little boy was able to catch a bush with one hand that hung over the bank, while holding on to his mother with the other, and so she was saved.

"It was then nearly dark, and without any knowledge of how far it was to camp, the little party started on the road, only tarrying long enough on the bank of the river for the mother to wring the water out of her skirts, the boy carrying the baby while the four-year-old walked beside his mother. After nearly two miles of travel and ascending a very steep hill, it being now dark, the glimmer of camp lights came in view; but the mother could see nothing, for she fell senseless, utterly prostrated.

"I have been up and down that hill a number of times, and do not wonder the poor woman fell senseless after the effort to reach the top. The great wonder is that she should have been able to go as far as she did. The incident illustrates how the will power can nerve one up to extraordinary achievements, but when the object is attained and the danger is past, then the power is measureably lost, as in this case, when the good woman came to know they were safe. The boy hurried his two little brothers into camp, calling for help to rescue his mother. The appeal was promptly responded to, the woman being carried into camp and tenderly cared for until she revived.

"Being asked if he did not want something to eat, the boy said 'he had forgot all about it,' and further, 'he didn't see anything to eat, anyway;' whereupon some one with a stick began to uncover some roasted potatoes, which he has decided was the best meal he has ever eaten, even to this day.

"This is a plain recital of actual occurrences, without exaggeration, obtained from the parties themselves and corroborated by numerous living witnesses.

"There were 128 people in that train, and through the indefatigable efforts of Mr. Geo. H. Himes, of Portland, Oregon, who was one of the party, and in fact the ten-year-old boy referred to, I am able to give the names in part.

"I have been thus particular in telling this story to illustrate what trials were encountered and overcome by the pioneers of that day, to the end that the later generations may pause in their hasty condemnation of their present surroundings and opportunities and to ask themselves whether in all candor they do not feel they are blessed beyond the generation that has gone before them, the hardy pioneers of this country.

This book could easily be filled by the recital of such heroic acts, varying only in detail and perhaps in tragic results; yet would only show in fact the ready, resourceful tact of the pioneers of those days.

I want to repeat here again that I do not look upon that generation of men and women as superior to the present generation, except in this: The pioneers had lost a large number of physically weak on the trip, thus applying the great law of the survival of the fittest; and further, that the great number were pioneers in the true sense of the word—frontiersmen for generations before —hence were by training and habits eminently fitted to meet the emergencies of the trip and conditions to follow.

One of the incidents of this trip should be related to perpetuate the memory of heroic actions of the times, that of the famous ride across these mountains and to Olympia, of Mrs. Catherine Frazier, one of this party, on an ox.

Three days after arrival, Mrs. Frazier gave birth to the third white child born in Pierce County, Washington Frazier, named after the great territory that had been chosen for the home of the parents and descendants.

The first report, that the "mother and son were doing well," can again and again be repeated, as both * are yet alive, the mother now past seventy-three and the son fifty, and both yet residing at South Bay, near Olympia, where the parents settled soon after arrival.

The curious part of such incidents is the perfect unconsciousness of the parties, of having done anything

---

*Since these lines were penned Mrs. Frazier has joined the majority of that generation in the life beyond.

that would be handed down to posterity as exhibiting any spirit of fortitude or of having performed any heroic act. The young bride could not walk, neither could she be taken into the wagons, and she *could* ride an ox, and so without ceremony, mounted her steed and fell into the procession without attracting especial attention or passing remark. Doubtless the lady, at the time, would have shrunk from any undue notice, because of her mount, and would have preferred a more appropriate entry into the future capitol of the future State, but it is now quite probable that she looks upon the act with a feeling akin to pride, and in any event, not with feelings of mortification or false pride that possibly, at the time, might have lurked within her breast.

The birth of children was not an infrequent incident on the plains, the almost universal report following, "doing as well as could be expected," the trip being resumed with but very short interruption, the little ones being soon exhibited with the usual motherly pride.

CHAPTER XIII.

Trip Through the Natchess Pass—Continued.

Readers of previous chapters will remember the lonely camp mentioned and the steep mountain ahead of it to reach the summit.

What with the sweat incident to the day's travel, the chill air of an October night in the mountains, with but half of a three-point blanket as covering and the ground for a mattress, small wonder my muscles were a little stiffened when I arose and prepared for the ascent to the summit. Bobby had, as I have said, been restless during the night, and, when the roll of blankets and the hard bread was securely strapped on behind, suddenly turned his face homeward, evidently not relishing the fare of browse for supper. He seemingly had concluded he had had enough of the trip, and started to go home, trotting off gaily down the mountain. I could do nothing else but follow him, as the narrow cut of the road and impenetrable obstructions on either side utterly precluded my getting past to head off his rascally maneuvers. Finally, finding a nip of grass by the roadside, the gait was slackened so that after several futile attempts I managed to get a firm hold of his tail, after which we went down the mountain together much more rapidly than we had come up the evening before. Bobby forgot to use his heels, else he might for a longer time been master of the situation. The fact was, he did not want to hurt me, but was determined to break up the partnership, and, so far as he was concerned, go no further into the mountains where he could not get a supper. By dint of persuasion and main strength of muscle the contest was finally settled in my favor, and I secured the rein. Did I chastise him? Not a bit. I did not blame him. We were partners, but it was a one-sided partnership, as he had no interest in the enterprise other

than to get enough to eat as we went along, and when
that failed, rebelled.

It is wonderful, the sagacity of the horse or ox. They
know more than we usually think they do. Let one be
associated (yes, that's the word, associated), with them
for a season alone. Their characteristics come to the
front and become apparent without study. Did I talk
to my friend, Bobby? Indeed, I did. There were but
few other animate things to talk to. Perhaps one might
see a small bird flit across the vision or a chipmunk, or
hear the whirr of the sudden flight of the grouse, but all
else was solitude, deep and impressive. The dense forest through which I was passing did not supply conditions for bird or animal life in profusion.

"You are a naughty lad, Bobby," I said, as I turned
his head eastward to retrace the mile or so of the truant's
run.

We were soon past our camping ground of the night
before, and on our way up the mountain. Bobby would
not be led, or if he was, would hold back, till finally
making a rush up the steep ascent, would be on my heels
or toes before I could get out of the way. "Go ahead,
Bobby," I would say, and suiting action to words seize
the tail with a firm grasp and follow. When he moved
rapidly, by holding on, I was helped up the mountain.
When he slackened his pace, then came the resting spell.
The engineering instinct of the horse tells him how to
reduce grades by angles. So Bobby led me up the mountain in zig-zag courses, I following always, with the
firm grasp of the tail that meant we would not part
company, and we did not. I felt that it was a mean trick
to compel the poor brute to pull me up the mountain
by his tail, supperless, breakfastless, and discontented.
It appeared to me it was just cause to sever our friendship, which by this time seemed cemented closely, but
then I thought of the attempted abandonment he had
been guilty of, and that perhaps he should submit to
some indignities at my hand in consequence.

By noon we had surmounted all obstacles, and stood upon the summit prairie—one of them, for there are several—where Bobby feasted to his heart's content, while I—well, it was the same old story, hard tack and cheese, with a small allotment of dried venison.

To the south apparently but a few miles distant, the old mountain, Rainier of old, Tacoma by Winthrop, loomed up into the clouds full ten thousand feet higher than where I stood, a grand scene to behold, worthy of all the effort expended to attain this view point. But I was not attuned to view with ecstasy the grandeur of what lay before me, but rather to scan the horizon to ascertain if I could, what the morrow might bring forth. The mountain to the pioneer has served as a huge barometer to foretell the weather. "How is the mountain this morning?" the farmer asks in harvest time. "Has the mountain got his night cap on?" the housewife inquires before her wash is hung on the line. The Indian would watch the mountain with intent to determine whether he might expect *"snass"* (rain), or *"kull snass"* (hail), or *"t'kope snass"* (snow), and seldom failed in his conclusions, and so I scanned the mountain top that day partially hid in the clouds, with forebodings verified at night fall, as will be related later.

The next camp was in the Natchess Canyon. I had lingered on the summit prairie to give the pony a chance to fill up on the luxuriant but rather washy grass, there found in great abundance. For myself, I had had plenty of water, but had been stinted in hard bread, remembering my experience of the day before, with the famishing women and children. I began to realize more and more, the seriousness of my undertaking, particularly so, because I could hear no tidings. A light snow storm came on just before nightfall, which, with the high mountains on either side of the river, spread approaching darkness rapidly. I was loth to camp; somehow I just wanted to go on, and doubtless would have traveled all

night if I could have safely found my way. The canyon
was but a few hundred yards wide, with the tortuous
river first striking one bluff and then the other, neces-
sitating- numerous crossings; the intervening space
being glade land of large pine growth with but light
undergrowth and few fallen trees. The whole surface
was covered with coarse sand, in which rounded boulders
were imbedded so thick in places as to cause the trail
to be very indistinct, particularly in open spots, where
the snow had fallen unobstructed. Finally, I saw that
I must camp, and after crossing the river, came out in
an opening where the bear tracks were so thick that
one could readily believe the spot to be a veritable play
ground for all the animals round about.

I found two good sized trunks of trees that had fallen;
one obliquely across the other, and, with my pony tethered as a sentinel and my fire as an advance post, I
slept soundly, but nearly supperless. The black bears
on the west slope of the mountain I knew were timid
and not dangerous, but I did not know so much about
the mountain species, and can but confess that I felt
lonesome, though placing great reliance upon my fire,
which I kept burning all night

Early next morning found Bobby and me on the trail,
a little chilled with the cold mountain air and very willing to travel. In a hundred yards or so, we came upon
a ford of ice cold water to cross, and others following
in such quick succession, that I realized that we were
soon to leave the canyon. I had been told that at the
32nd crossing I would leave the canyon and ascend a
high mountain, and then travel through pine glades,
and that I must then be careful and not lose the trail.
I had not kept strict account of the crossings like one
of the men I had met, who cut a notch in his goad stick
at every crossing, but I knew instinctively we were
nearly out, and so I halted to eat what I supposed would
be the only meal of the day, not dreaming what lay in

store for me at nightfall. It would be uninteresting to the general reader to relate the details of that day's travel, and in fact I cannot recall much about it, except going up the steep mountain; so steep that Bobby again practiced his engineering instincts and I mine, with my selfish hand having a firm hold of the tail of my now patient comrade.

From the top of the mountain grade I looked back in wonderment about how the immigrants had taken their wagons down; I found out by experience afterwards.

Toward nightfall I heard a welcome sound of the tinkling of a bell, and soon saw the smoke of camp fires, and finally the village of tents and grime covered wagons. How I tugged at Bobby's halter to make him go faster, and then mounted him with not much better results, can better be imagined than told.

Could it be the camp I was searching for? It was about the number of wagons and tents that I had expected to meet. No. I was doomed to disappointment, yet rejoiced to find some one to camp with and talk to other than the pony.

It is not easy to describe the cordial greeting accorded me by those tired and almost discouraged immigrants. If we had been near and dear relatives, the rejoicing could not have been mutually greater. They had been toiling for nearly five months on the road across the plains, and now there loomed up before them this great mountain range to cross. Could they do it? If we cannot get over with our wagons, can we get the women and children through in safety? I was able to lift a load of doubt and fear from off their jaded minds. Before I knew what was happenning, I caught the fragrance of boiling coffee and of fresh meat cooking. It seemed the good matrons knew without telling that I was hungry (I doubtless looked it), and had set to work to prepare me a meal, a sumptuous meal at that, taking into account the whetted appetite incident to a diet of hard bread straight, and not much of that either, for two days.

We had met on the hither bank of the Yakima River, where the old trail crosses that river near where the flourishing city of North Yakima now is. These were the people, a part of them, that are mentioned elsewhere in the chapter on the White River massacre. Harvey H. Jones, wife and three children, and George E. King, wife and one child. One of the little boys of the camp is the same person—John I. King—who has written the graphic account of the tragedy that follows, in which his mother and step father and their neighbors lost their lives—that horrible massacre on White River a year later, and the other, George E. King, (but no relation) the little five-year-old who was taken and held captive for nearly four months, and then safely delivered over by the Indians to the military authorities at Fort Steilacoom. I never think of those people but with feelings of sadness; of their struggle, doubtless the supreme effort of their lives, to go to their death. I pointed out to them where to go to get good claims, and they lost no time, but went straight to the locality recommended and immediately to work, preparing shelter for the winter.

"Are you going out on those plains alone?" asked Mrs. Jones, anxiously. When informed that I would have the pony with me, a faint, sad smile spread over her countenance as she said, "Well, I don't think it is safe." Mr. Jones explained that what his wife referred to was the danger from the ravenous wolves that infested the open country, and from which they had lost weakened stock from their bold forages, "right close to the camp," he said, and advised me not to camp near the watering places, but up on the high ridge. I followed his advice with the result as we shall see of missing my road and losing considerable time, and causing me not a little trouble and anxiety.

CHAPTER XIV.

Trip Through the Natchess Pass—Continued.

The start for the high table desert lands bordering the Yakima valley cut me loose from all communication, for no more immigrants were met until I reached the main traveled route beyond the Columbia River. I speak of the "desert lands" adjacent to the Yakima from the standpoint of that day. We all thought these lands were worthless, as well as the valley, not dreaming of the untold wealth the touch of water would bring out. The road lay through a forbidding sage plain, or rather an undulating country, seemingly of shifting sands and dead grass of comparatively scant growth. As the sun rose the heat became intolerable. The dust brought vivid memories of the trip across the plains in places. The heated air trembling in the balance brought the question of whether or not something was the matter with my eyes or brain; whether this was an optical illusion, or real, became a debatable question in my mind. Strive against it with all my might, my eyes would rest on the farther horizon to catch the glimpse of the expected train, till they fairly ached. Added to this, an intolerable thirst seized upon me, and compelled leaving the road and descending into the valley for water. Here I found as fat cattle as ever came to a butcher's stall, fed on this self same dead grass, cured without rain. These cattle belonged to the Indians, but there were no Indians in sight. The incident, though, set me to thinking about the possibilities of a country that could produce such fat cattle from the native grasses. I must not linger off the trail, and take chances of missing the expected train, and so another stretch of travel, of thirst, and suffering came until during the afternoon, I found water on the trail, and tethered my pony for his much needed dinner, and opened my sack of hard bread to count the contents, with the conclusion that my store was half gone, and so lay down in the shade of a small tree or bush near the spring to take an afternoon nap. Rousing up before sun down, refreshed, we (pony and I), took the trail in a much better mood than before the nooning. When night came, I could not find it in my heart to camp. The cool of the evening invigorated the pony, and we pushed on. Without having intended to travel in the night, I had, so to speak, drifted into it and finding the road could be followed, though but dimly seen, kept on the way until a late hour, when I unsaddled and hobbled the pony. The saddle blanket was brought into use, and I was soon off in dream land, and forgot all about the dust, the train or the morrow.

Morning brought a puzzling sense of helplessness that for the time, seemed overpowering. I had slept late, and awoke to find the pony had wandered far off on the hill side, in fact, so far, it required close scanning to discover him. To make matters worse, his hobbles had became loosened, giving him free use of all his feet, and in no mood to take the trail again. Coaxing was of no avail, driving would do no good, so embracing an opportunity to seize his tail again, we went around about over the plain and through the sage brush in a rapid gait, which finally lessened and I again became master of him. For the life of me I could not be sure as to the direction of the trail, but happened to take the right course. When the trail was found, the question came as to the whereabouts of the saddle. It so happened that I took the wrong direction and had to retrace my steps. The sun was high when we started on our journey.

A few hundred yards travel brought feelings of uneasiness, as it was evident that we were not on the regular trail. Not knowing but this was some cut off,

so continued until the Columbia River bluff was reached, and the great river was in sight, half a mile distant,
and several hundred feet of lower level.   Taking a trail
down the bluff that seemed more promising than the
wagon tracks, I began to search for the road at the foot
of the bluff to find the tracks scattered, and any resem-
blance of a road gone; in a word, I was lost.   I never
knew how those wagon tracks came to be there, but I
know that I lost more than a half day's precious time,
and again was thrown in a doubting mood as to whether
I had missed the long sought for train.

The next incident I remember vividly, was my attempt
to cross the Columbia just below the mouth of Snake
River.   I had seen but very few Indians on the whole trip,
and in fact, the camp I found there on the bank of the
great river was the first I distinctly remember.   I could
not induce them to cross me over.   From some cause
they seemed surly and unfriendly.   The treatment was
so in contrast to what I had received from the Indians
on the Sound, that I could not help wondering what it
meant.   No one, to my knowledge, lost his life by the
hands of the Indians that season, but the next summer
all, or nearly all, were ruthlessly murdered that ven-
tured into that country unprotected.

That night I camped late, opposite Wallula (old Fort
Walla Walla), in a sand storm of great fury.   I tethered
my pony this time, rolled myself up in the blanket, only
to find myself fairly buried in the drifting sand in the
morning.   It required a great effort to creep out of the
blanket, and greater work to relieve the blanket from the
accumulated sand.   By this time the wind had laid and
comparative calm prevailed, and then came the effort to
make myself heard across the wide river to the people
of the fort.   It did seem as though I would fail.   Traveling up and down the river bank for half a mile, or so,
in the hopes of catching a favorable breeze to carry
my voice to the fort, yet, all to no avail.   I sat upon the

bank hopelessly discouraged, not knowing what to do. I think I must have been two hours halloaing at the top of my voice until hoarse from the violent effort. Finally, while sitting there, cogitating as to what to do, I spied a blue smoke arising from the cabin, and soon after a man appeared who immediately responded to my renewed efforts to attract attention. The trouble had been they were all asleep, while I was in the early morning expending my breath.

Shirley Ensign, of Olympia, had established a ferry across the Columbia River, and had yet lingered to set over belated immigrants, if any came. Mr. Ensign came over and gave me glad tidings. He had been out on the trail fifty miles or more, and had met my people, whom he thought were camped some thirty miles away, and thought that they would reach the ferry on the following day. But I would not wait, and, procuring a fresh horse, I started out in a cheerful mood, determined to reach camp that night if my utmost exertions would accomplish it. Sundown came and no signs of camp; dusk drew on, and still no signs; finally, I spied some cattle grazing on the upland, and soon came upon the camp in a ravine that had shut them out from view. Rejoicing and outbursts of grief followed. I inquired for my mother the first thing. She was not there; had been buried in the sands of the Platte Valley, months before; also a younger brother lay buried near Independence rock. The scene that followed is of too sacred memory to write about, and we will draw the veil of privacy over it.

Of that party, all are under the sod save two—Mrs. Lulu Packard, now of Portland, Oregon, and Mrs. Amanda C. Spinning, then the wife of the elder brother so often heretofore mentioned.

With fifty odd head of stock, seven wagons, and seventeen people, the trip was made to the Sound without serious mishap or loss. We were twenty-two days on the road, and thought this was good time to make, all things considered. Provisions were abundant, the health of the party good, and stock in fair condition. I unhesitatingly advised the over-mountain trip; meanwhile cautioning them to expect some snow, a goodly amount of hard labor, and plenty of vexation. How long will it take? Three weeks. Why, we thought we were about through. Well, you came to stay with us, did you? But what about the little wife and the two babies on the island home? Father said some one must go and look after them. So, the elder brother was detailed to go to the island folks, whilst I was impressed into service to take his place with the immigrants. It would hardly be interesting to the general reader to give a detailed account, even if I remembered it well, which I do not. So intent did we all devote our energies to the one object, to get safely over the mountains, that all else was forgotten. It was a period of severe toil and anxious care, but not more so than to others that had gone before us, and what others had done we felt we could do, but there was no eight-hour-a-day labor, nor any drones; all were workers. I had prepared the minds of the new-comers for the worst, not forgetting the steep hills, the notched logs, and rough, stony fords, by telling the whole story. But do you really think we can get through? said father. Yes, I know we can, if every man will put his shoulder to the wheel. This latter expression was a phrase in use to indicate doing one's duty without flinching, but in this case, it had a more literal meaning, for we were compelled often to take hold of the wheels to boost the wagons over logs, and ease them down on the opposite side, as likewise, on the steep mountain side. We divided our force into groups; one to each wagon to drive, four as wheelmen as we called them, and father with the women folks on foot, or on horseback, with the stock.

God bless the women folks of the plains; the immi-

grant women, I mean. A nobler, braver, more uncom-
plaining people were never known. I have often thought
that some one ought to write a just tribute to their
valor and patience; a book of their heroic deeds. I
know this word valor, is supposed to apply to men and
not to women, but I know that the immigrant women
earned the right to have the word, and all it implies,
applied to them. Such a trip with all its trials is almost
worth the price to bring out these latent virtues of the
so called weaker sex. Strive, however, as best we could,
we were unable to make the trip in the alloted time, and
willing hands came out with the brother to put *their*
shoulders to the wheels, and to bring the glad tidings
that all was well on the island home, and to release the
younger brother and the father from further duty, when
almost through to the settlements.

Do you say this was enduring great hardships? That
depends upon the point of view. As to this return trip,
for myself, I can truly say that it was not. I enjoyed
the strife to overcome all difficulties, and so did the
greater number of the company. They felt that it was
a duty and enjoyed doing their duty. Many of them,
it is true, were weakened by the long trip across the
plains, but with the better food obtainable, and the goal
so near at hand, there was a positive pleasure to pass
over the miles, one by one, and become assured that
final success was only a matter of a very short time.

One day, we encountered a new fallen tree, as one
of the men said, a whopper, cocked up on its own upturned roots, four feet from the ground. Go around it,
we could not; to cut it out seemed an endless task
with our dulled, flimsy saw. Dig down, boys, said the
father, and in short order every available shovel was
out of the wagons and into willing hands, with others
standing by to take their turn. In a short time the way
was open fully four feet deep, and oxen and wagons
passed through under the obstruction.

CHAPTER XV.

Trip Through the Natchess Pass—Continued.

People now traversing what is popularly known as Nisqually Plains, that is, the stretch of open prairie, interpersed with clumps of timber, sparkling lakes, and glade lands, from the heavy timber bordering the Puyallup to a like border of the Nisqually, will hardly realize that once upon a time these bare gravelly prairies supplied a rich grass of exceeding fattening quality of sufficient quantity to support many thousand head of stock, and not only support but fatten them ready for the butcher's stall. Nearly half a million acres of this land lie between the two rivers, from two to four hundred feet above tide level and beds of the rivers mentioned, undulating and in benches, an ideal park of shade and open land of rivulets and lakes, of natural roads and natural scenery of splendor.

So, when our little train emerged from the forests skirting the Puyallup Valley, and came out on the open at Montgomery's, afterwards Camp Montgomery, of Indian war times, twelve miles southeasterly of Fort Steilacoom, the experience was almost as if one had come into a noonday sun from a dungeon prison, so marked was the contrast. Hundreds of cattle, sheep and horses were quietly grazing, scattered over the landscape, as far as one could see, fat and content. It is not to be wondered that the spirits of the tired party should rise as they saw this scene of content before them, and thought they could become participants with those who had come before them, and that for the moment rest was theirs if that was what they might choose.

Fort Nisqually was about ten miles south-westerly from our camp at Montgomery's, built, as mentioned elsewhere, by the Hudson Bay Company, in 1833.

In 1840-41, this company's holdings at Nisqually and Cowlitz were transfered to the Puget Sound Agricultural Company. This latter company was organized in London at the instance of Dr. Wilham F. Tolmie, who visited that city to conduct the negotiations in person with the directors of the Hudson Bay Company. He returned clothed with the power to conduct the affairs of the new company, but under the direction of the Hudson Bay Company, and with the restriction not to enter into or interfere with the fur trade; he later became the active agent of both companies at Nisqually.

It was principally the stock of this company that we saw from our camp and near by points. At that time, the Agricultural Company had several farms on these plains, considerable pasture land enclosed, and four-teen thousand head of stock running at large; sheep, cattle, and horses.

The United States government actually paid rent to this foreign company for many years for the site where Fort Steilacoom was located for account of the shadowy title of the company under the treaty of 1846.

During this lapse of time, from 1833 to the time our camp was established, many of the company's servants time had expired and in almost every case, such had taken to themselves Indian wives and had squatted on the choice locations for grazing or small farming. Mont-gomery himself, near whose premises we were camping, was one of these. A few miles to the south of this place, ran the small creek "Muck," on the surface for several miles to empty into the Nisqually. Along this little creek, others of these discharged servants had settled, and all taken Indian wives. These were the settlers that were afterwards denounced by Governor Stevens, and finally arrested for alleged treason, as is fully set out in other chapters. Each of these had abundance of stock and farm produce, and was living in affluence and comfort. One of these, reputed to be the rightful owner of thirteen cows, one summer raised thirty-three calves, the handy lasso rope having been brought into play among the company's herds in secluded places; yet, as the rule, these people were honorable, upright men, though as a class, not of high intelligence, or of sober habits.

Added to this class just mentioned, was another; the discharged United States soldiers. The men then comprising the United States army were far below in moral worth and character than now. Many of these men had also taken Indian wives and settled where they had chosen to select. Added to these were a goodly number of the previous years' immigrants. By this recital the reader will be apprised of the motley mess our little party were destined to settle among, unless they should choose to go to other parts of the Territory. I did not myself fully realize the complications to be met until later years.

All this while, as we have said, settlers were crowding into the district, taking up donation claims until that act expired by limitation in 1854, and afterwards by squatter's rights, which to all appearances, seemed as good as any. My own donation claim afterwards was involved in this controversy, in common with many others. Although our proofs of settlement were made and all requirements of the law complied with, nevertheless, our patents were held up and our title questioned for twenty years, and so, after having made the trip across the plains, because Uncle Sam had promised to give us all a farm, and after having made the required improvements and resided on the land for the four years, then to be crowded off without title did seem a little rough on the pioneers.

I have before me one of the notices served upon the

settlers by the company's agent which tells the whole story.* The then thriving town of Steilacoom was involved, as likewise part of the lands set apart for the Indian Reservation, and it did seem as though it would be hard to get a more thorough mix-up as to titles of the land, than these knotty questions presented.

All this while, as was natural there should be, there was constant friction between some settler and the company, and had it not been for the superior tact of such a man as Dr. Tolmie in charge of the company's affairs, there would have been serious trouble.

As it was, there finally came a show of arms when the company undertook to survey the boundary line to inclose the land claimed, although the acreage was much less than claimed on paper. But the settlers, (or some of them), rebelled, and six of them went armed to the party of surveyors at work and finally stopped them. An old-time friend, John McLeod, was one of the party (mob, the company called it), but the records do not show whether he read his chapter in the Bible that day, or whether instead, he took a double portion of whiskey to relieve his conscience.

It is doubtful whether the old man thought he was doing wrong or thought anything about it, except that he had a belief that somehow or other a survey might make against him getting a title to his own claim.

ORIGINAL WARNING TO THOMAS HADLEY.

We hereby certify that a correct copy of the within notice was presented to T. Hadley by Mr. Wm. Greig this 6th day of April, 1857.

WILLIAM GREIG.
ALFRED McNEILL.
AMBROSE SKINNER.

Nisqually, W. T., 12th March, 1857.

To Mr. Thomas Hadley.—Sir: I hereby warn you that, in cultivating land and making other improvements on your present location in or near the Talentire precinct, Pierce County, Washington Territory, you are trespassing on the lands confirmed to the Puget's Sound Agricultural Company by the Boundary Treaty, ratified in July, 1846, between Great Britain and the United States of America. Very Respectfully

Your Obed't Servt.,

W. F. TOLMIE.
Agent Puget's Sound Agricultural Company.

I had similar experience at a later date with the Indians near the Muckleshute Reservation, as elsewhere related, while attempting to extend the sub-divisional lines of the township near where the reserve was located. I could not convince the Indians that the survey meant no harm to them.

The case was different in the first instance, as in fact, neither party was acting within the limits of their legal rights, and for the time being, the strongest and most belligerent prevailed, but only to be circumvented at a little later date by a secret completion of the work, sufficient to platting the whole.

All this while the little party was halting. The father said the island home would not do, and as he had come two thousand miles to live neighbors, I must give up my claim and take another near theirs, and so, abandoning over a year's hard work, I acted upon his request with the result told elsewhere, of fleeing from our new chosen home, as we supposed, to save our lives, upon the outbreak of the Indian War in less than a year from the time of the camp mentioned.

One can readily see that these surroundings did not promise that compact, staid settlement of energetic, wide awake pioneers we so coveted, nevertheless, the promise of money returns was good, and that served to allay any discontent that would otherwise arise. I remember the third year we began selling eighteen months' old steers at fifty dollars each, off the range that had never been fed a morsel. Our butter sold for fifty cents a pound, and at times, seventy-five cents, and many other things at like prices. No wonder all hands soon became contented; did not have time to be otherwise.

It came about though, that we were in considerable part a community within ourselves, yet, there were many excellent people in the widely scattered settlements. The conditions to some extent encouraged lawlessness, and within the class already mentioned, a good deal of drunkenness and what one might well designate as loose morals, incident to the surroundings. A case in point:

A true, though one might say a humorous, story is told on Doctor Tolmie, or one of his men, of visiting a settler where they knew one of their beeves had been slaughtered and appropriated. To get direct evidence he put himself in the way of an invitation to dinner, where, sure enough, the fresh, fat beef was smoking on the table. The good old pioneer (I knew him well), asked a good, old-fashioned Methodist blessing over the meat, giving thanks for the bountiful supply of the many good things of the world vouchsafed to him and his neighbors, and thereupon in true pioneer hospitality, cut a generous sized piece of the roast for his guest, the real owner of the meat.

This incident occurred just as here related, and although the facts are as stated, yet we must not be too ready to scoff at our religious friend and condemn him without a hearing. To me, it would have been just as direct thieving as any act could have been, and yet, to our sanctified friend I think it was not, and upon which thereby hangs a tale.

Many of the settlers looked upon the company as interlopers, pure and simple, without any rights they were bound to respect. There had been large numbers of cattle and sheep run on the range and had eaten the feed down, which they thought was robbing them of their right of eminent domain for the land they claimed the government had promised to give them.

The cattle become very wild, in great part on account of the settlers' actions, but the curious part was they afterwards justified themselves from the fact that they were wild, and so it happened there came very near being claim of common property of the company's stock, with not a few of the settlers.

One lawless act is almost sure to breed another, and

there was no exception to the rule in this strange community, and many is the settler that can remember the disappearance of stock which could be accounted for in but one way—gone with the company's herd. In a few years, though, all this disappeared. The incoming immigrants from across the plains were a sturdy set as a class, and soon frowned down such a loose code of morals.

For a moment let us turn to the little camp on the edge of the prairie, of seven wagons and three tents. There came a time it must be broken up. No more camp fires, with the fragrant coffee morning and evening; no more smoking the pipe together over jests, or serious talk; no more tucks in the dresses of the ladies, compelled first by the exigencies of daily travel and now to be parted with under the inexorable law of custom or fashion; no more lumps of butter at night, churned during the day by the movement of wagon and the can containing the morning's milk. We must hie us off to prepare shelter from the coming storms of winter; to the care of the stock; the preparations for planting; to the beginning of a new life of independence.

CHAPTER XVI.

Trip Through the Natchess Pass—Concluded.

It almost goes without saying, that before the final break up of the camp and separation of the parties there must be some sort of a celebration of the event, a sort of house warming or surprise party—something must be done out of the usual course of events. So, what better could these people do than to visit the island * home they had heard so much about, and see for themselves some of the wonder land described.

My cabin stood on the south side of the bight or lagoon within stone throw of where the United States penitentiary now stands and only a few feet above high tide level. The lagoon widens and deepens from the entrance and curves to the south with gentle slope on either side, the whole forming a miniature sheltered valley of light, timbered, fertile land. On the higher levels of the receding shore, great quantities of the sallal and high bush huckleberries grew in profusion, interspersed with what for lack of a better name we called Sweet Bay, the perfumes from the leaves of which permeated the atmosphere for long distances. In the near by front a long flat or sandy beach extended far out from the high tide line where the clams spouted in countless numbers, and crows played their antics of breaking the shell by dropping to the stony beach the helpless bivalve they had stealthily clutched and taken to flight with them.

Off to the eastward and three miles distant the town of Steilacoom, or rather the two towns, loomed up like

*McNeil Island, twelve miles westerly as the crow flies from Tacoma.

quite a city, on the ascending slope of the shore, to make us feel after all we were not so far off from civilization, particularly at the time as two or more deep sea vessels, (ships we called them) were in port discharging merchandise. South-easterly, the grand mountain, before mentioned, rose so near three miles high above the tide level that that was the height spoken by all and as being fifty miles distant.

Nisqually House, on the arm of the bay known as Nisqually Reach, five miles distant, could be seen in clear weather, while the Hudson Bay Fort of that name was hidden from view by intervening timber, two miles easterly from the beach.

The Medicine Creek council grounds, afterwards made famous by the treaty council held a few months later than the date of which I am writing, lay across the Nisqually tide flats, south from Nisqually House, near three miles distant, but the view of this was cut off by an intervening island (Anderson), of several sections in extent, and of varying elevations to a maximum of near four hundred feet.

Fortunately one of those "spells" of weather had settled over the whole country, a veritable Indian Summer, though now bordering on the usually stormy month of November, a little hazy, just enough to lend enchantment to the landscape, and warm enough to add pleasurable experience to the trip the little party was to make. Add to these surroundings, the smooth glassy waters of the bay, interspersed here and there by streaks and spots of troubled water to vary the outlook, small wonder that enthusiasm ran high as the half-rested immigrants neared the cabin in their boat and canoe, chartered for the trip, piloted and paddled by the Indians and supplemented by the awkward stroke of the landlubber's oar.

"What in the world are we going to do with all these people?" I said to the little wife, half apologetically, partly quizzical and yet with a tinge of earnestness illy concealed.

"Oh, never mind, we will get along all right some way; I'll venture father has brought a tent." And sure enough, the party had brought the three tents that had served them so well for so long a time, on the long journey, and much of their bedding also.

Father had been over to the cabin before, and taken the measurement.

"Eighteen feet square," he said, "that's a pretty good size, but I don't see why you boys didn't build it higher; it's scant seven feet."

Yes, the walls were but seven feet high. When building, the logs ran out, the sky was threatening and we had a race with the storm to get a roof over our heads.

"But that's a good fireplace," he continued; "there must be pretty good clay here to hold these round stones so firmly. And that's as good a cat-and-clay chimney as I had in Ohio, only mine was taller, but I don't see that it would draw any better than this." This one was just nine feet high, but I said there was plenty of room to build it higher.

The floor was rough lumber, or had been when laid, but the stiff scrub brush of twigs and strong arms of house cleaners had worn off the rough till when cleaned it presented a quite creditable appearance. And the walls! "Why, you have a good library on these walls; all the reading matter right side up too; the Tribune is a great paper, indeed; you must have sent for it right away when you got here," and so I had, and continued steadily for eighteen years, and thereby hangs a tale, which, though a digression I will tell before writing more about our visitors.

Eighteen years after my arrival from across the plains in October, 1852, I made my first trip to the "States," to our old home and to New York. I had to go through

the mud to the Columbia River, then out over the dreaded bar to the Pacific Ocean, and to San Francisco, then
on a seven days' journey over the Central, Union Pacific
and connecting lines and sit bolt upright all the way—
no sleeper cars then, no diners either, that I remember
seeing. I remember I started from Olympia on this trip
the first week in December. Mr. —— Woodard of
Olympia suggested that we gather all the varieties of
flowers obtainable in the open air and that I press them
in the leaves of my pamphlets (presently to be mentioned), and in that way to dry and press them, so I
might exhibit the product of our wonderful mild climate
up to the month of December. We succeeded in getting
fifty-two varieties then in bloom in the open air, and
all were well dried and preserved when I arrived at
my original starting place, Eddyville, Iowa. Here, lov-
ing friends, Mrs. Elizabeth Male, (Aunt Lib, we call
her now) and a little sprightly youngster, Miss Molly
Male, the well-known teacher in Tacoma, artistically arranged my treasures on tinted paper ready for exhibition upon my arrival in New York.

I had written an eighty page pamphlet (long since
out of print), descriptive of Washington Territory, and
my friend E. T. Gunn, of the Olympia Transcript, printed them—five thousand copies—most of which I took
with me. The late Beriah Brown gave me a letter of
introduction to his old-time friend, Horace Greeley, to
whom I presented it and was kindly received and com-
mended to chairman Ely of the New York Farmer's
Club, and by him given an opportunity to exhibit my
flowers, speak to the club about our country and tell
them about our climate. This little talk was widely
circulated through the proceedings of the club printed
in a number of the great papers, among them the
Tribune.

This coming to the notice of Jay Cooke, of Northern
Pacific fame, with his six power presses just started at

Philadelphia to advertise the Northern Pacific route, I was called to his presence and closely questioned, and finally complimented by the remark that he "did not think they could afford to have any opposition in the field of advertising," took up my whole edition and sent them on their way to his various financial agencies.

In the chapter, "The Morning School," the sequel to this story will be given, and so now we must return to the party at the island home.

Our visitors were all soon at home with their tents up, their blankets out airing, the camp fires lit and with an abandon truly refreshing turned out like children from school to have a good time. The garden, of course, was drawn upon and "such delicious vegetables I never saw before," fell from a dozen lips, during the stay. That turnip patch was planted in September. "Why, that beats anything I *ever* saw," father said, and as insignificent an incident as it may seem, had a decided effect upon the minds of the party. "Why, here they are growing in November. At home (Iowa) they would by this time be frozen as solid as a brick." "Why, these are the finest flavored potatoes I *ever* saw," said another. The little wife had a row of sweet peas growing near by the cabin that shed fragrance to the innermost corner and to the tents, and supplied bouquets for the tables, and plenty of small talk comparing them with those "in the States."

And so the little garden, the sweet peas, and other flowers wild and cultivated, brought contentment among those who at first had had a feeling of despondency and disappointment.

Didn't we have clam bakes? I should say! And didn't the women folks come in loaded with berries? And, what whoppers of huckleberry puddings, and huckleberry pies and all sorts of good things that ingenuity of the housewives could conjure up.

I had frequently seen deer trotting on the beach
and told my visitors so, but somehow they could not
so readily find them—had been too noisy, but soon a
fat buck was bagged, and the cup of joy was full, the
feast was on.

My visitors could not understand, and neither could
I, how it came that a nearby island (Anderson) of a few
sections in extent, could contain a lake of clear, fresh
water several hundred feet above tide level, and that
this lake should have neither inlet nor outlet. It was on
the margin of this lake that the first deer was killed and
nearby where the elder brother had staked his claim.

Mowich Man, an Indian whom I have known for many
years, and, by the way, one of those interfering with
the survey of Muckleshute, as related elsewhere, was
then one of our neighbors, or at least, frequently passed
our cabin with his canoe and people. He was a great
hunter, a crack shot, and an all round Indian of good
parts, by the standard applicable to his race. Many is
the saddle of venison that this man has brought me in
the lapse of years. He was not a man of any particular force of character, but his steadfast friendship has
always impressed me as to the worth, from our own
standpoint, of this race to which he belonged. While
our friends were with us visiting, my Indian friend came
along and as usual brought a nice ham of venison to
the camp, and at my suggestion, went with the
younger men of the visitors to where their first exploit
of hunting bore fruit. Our young men came back with
loud praise on their lips for the Indian hunter. There
was nothing specially noteworthy in the incident only
as illustrating what, to a great extent, was going on all
over the settled portion of the Territory leading up to a
better understanding between the two races. I can
safely say that none of the pioneers was without what
might be designated as a favorite Indian, that is, an
Indian who was particular to gain the good will of his

chosen friend, and in most cases would assume, or custom would bring about, the adoption of the white man's
name and the Indian would ever afterwards be known
by his new name. Mowich Man, however, like Leschi.
as we shall see later, while friendly to the whites was
possessed of a more independent spirit. Some of Mowich Man's people were fine singers, and in fact his
camp, or his canoe if traveling, was always the center
for song and merriment, but it is a curious fact one
seldom can get the Indian music by asking for it, but
rather must wait for its spontaneous outburst. But
Indian songs in those days came out from nearly every
nook and corner and seemed to pervade the whole country, so much that we often and often could hear the songs
and accompanying stroke of the paddle long before our
eyes would rest on the floating canoes.

Will the reader in his mind dwell on the hardships of
the pioneers, or will he rather look upon the brighter
side, that the so called hardships were simply the drill
that developed the manhood and womanhood, to make
better men and better women, because they had faced
a duty they could not shirk, and were thereby profited?
Neither did the pioneers as a class want to shirk a
duty and those of the later generation who have poured
out their sympathy for the hardships of the poor pioneers may as well save some of it for the present generation, the drones of the community that see no pleasure
in the stern duties of life. But I must have done with
these reflections to resume my story, now nearly ended,
of the visitors at the island home and of the long trip.

Never did kings or queens enjoy their palaces more,
nor millionaires their princely residences, than the
humble immigrant party did the cabin and tents in
their free and luxurious life. Queens might have their
jewels, but did we not have ours? Did we not have our
two babies, "the nicest, smartest, cutest in all the
world?" Did we not have a profusion of fresh air to

inhale at every breath, and appetites that made every morsel of food of exquisite flavor?

But we were all far away from what all yet thought of as home, and admonished that winter was coming on and that after a short season of recreation and rest we must separate, each to his task, and which we did, and the great trip was ended. The actors separated; and now, as I write, almost all have gone on that greater journey, in which the three of us left are so soon to join.

CHAPTER XVII.

The First Immigrants Through the Natchess Pass, 1853.

While the breaking of the barrier of the great mountain range for the immigrants to Puget Sound through the Natchess Pass was not in a baptism of blood, certainly it was under the stress of great suffering and anxiety, as shown by the graphic letter following, of that indefatigable worker and painstaking searcher after historic facts, Geo. H. Himes, now of Portland, Oregon, the real father of that great institution, the Oregon State Historical Society.

Having, as the reader will see by the reading of other chapters of this work, had some keen personal experiences through this gap of the mountains, it is but natural the incidents will come nearer home to me than to the general reader, particularly as I know the sincerity of purpose of the writer and the utter absence of any spirit of exaggeration. Although some errors have crept into Mr. Himes' letter, where he has drawn from other sources, yet this in nowise detracts from the value of his statement, but shows how very difficult it is to ascertain exact facts so long after the events.

The letter follows:

"Portland, Oregon, Jan. 23, 1905.
"My Dear Meeker:

"Some time early in August, 1853, Nelson Sargent, from Puget Sound, met our party in Grand Ronde valley, saying to his father, Asher Sargent, mother, two sisters and two brothers, and such others as he could make an impression on, 'You want to go to Puget Sound. That is a better country than the Willamette valley. All the good land is taken

EDWARD JAY ALLEN, 1853.   NELSON SARGENT, 1849.   BREAKING THE BARRIER
THROUGH THE NATCHESS PASS.

up there; but in the Sound region you can have the pick of the best. The settlers on Puget Sound have cut a road through Natchess Pass, and you can go direct from the Columbia through the Cascade Mountains, and thus avoid the wearisome trip through the mountains over the Barlow route to Portland, and then down the Columbia to Cowlitz River, and then over a miserable road to Puget Sound.'

"A word about the Sargents. Asher Sargent and his son Nelson left Indiana in 1849 for California. The next year they drifted northward to the northern part of Oregon—Puget Sound. Some time late in 1850 Nelson and a number of others were shipwrecked on Queen Charlotte Island, and remained among the savages for several months. The father, not hearing from the son, supposed he was lost, and in 1851 returned to Indiana. Being rescued in time, Nelson wrote home that he was safe; so in the spring of 1853 the Sargents, Longmire, Van Ogle, and possibly some others from Indiana, started for Oregon. Somewhere on the Platte the Biles (two families), Bakers (two families), Downeys, Kincaids, my father's family (Tyrus Himes), John Dodge and family—John Dodge did the stone work on the original Territorial university building at Seattle; Tyrus Himes was the first boot and shoemaker north of the Columbia River; James Biles was the first tanner, and a lady, Mrs. Frazier, was the first milliner and dressmaker—all met and journeyed westward peaceably together, all bound for Willamette valley. The effect of Nelson Sargent's presence and portrayal of the magnificent future of Puget Sound, caused most members of this company of 140 or more persons—or the leaders thereof, James Biles being the most conspicuous—to follow his (Sargent's) leadership. At length the Umatilla camp ground was reached, which was situated about three miles below the present city of Pendleton. From that point the company headed for old Fort Walla Walla (Wallula of to-day), on the Columbia River. It was understood that there would be no difficulty in crossing, but no boat was found. Hence a flatboat was made by whipsawing lumber out of driftwood. Then we went up the Yakima River, crossing it eight times. Then to the Natchess River, through the sage brush, frequently as high as a covered wagon, which had to be cut down before we could pass through it. On Sept. 15th we reached the mountains and found that there was no road, nothing but an Indian trail to follow. Indeed, there was no road whatever after leaving the Columbia, and nothing but a trail from the Umatilla to the Columbia; but being an open country, we had no particular difficulty in making headway. But I remember all hands felt quite serious the night we camped in the edge of the timber—the first of any consequence that we had seen—on the night of the 15th of September. Sargent said he knew the settlers had started to make a road, and could not understand why it was not completed; and since his parents, brothers and sisters were in the company, most of us believed that he did not intend to deceive. However, there was no course to pursue but to go forward. So we pushed on as best we could, following the bed of the stream part of the time, first on one bank and then on the other. Every little ways we would reach a point too difficult to pass; then we would go to the high ground and cut our way through the timber, frequently not making more than two or three miles a day. Altogether, the Natchess was crossed sixty-eight times. On this journey there was a stretch of fifty miles without a blade of grass—the sole subsistence of cattle and horses being browse from young maple and alder trees, which was not very filling, to say the least. In making the road every person from ten years old up lent a hand, and there is where your humble servant had his first lessons in trail-making, barefooted to boot, but not much, if any, worse off than many others. It was certainly a strenuous time for the women, and many were the forebodings indulged in as to the probability of getting safely through. One woman, 'Aunt Pop,' as she was called—one of the Woolery women—would break down and shed tears now and then; but in the midst of her weeping she would rally and by some quaint remark or funny story would cause everybody in her vicinity to forget their troubles.

"In due time the summit of the Cascades was reached. Here there was a small prairie—really, it was an old burn that had not grown up to timber of any size. Now it was October, about the 8th of the month, and bitter cold to the youth with bare feet and fringed pants extending half way down from knees to feet. My father and the teams had left camp and gone across the little burn, where most of the company was assembled, apparently debating about the next movement to make. And no wonder; for as we came across we saw the cause of the delay. For a sheer thirty feet or more there was an almost perpendicular bluff, and the only way to go forward was by that way, as was demonstrated by an examination all about the vicinity. Heavy timber at all other points precluded the possibility of getting on by any other route. So the longest rope in the company was stretched down the cliff, leaving just enough to be used twice around a small tree which stood on the brink of the precipice; but it was found to be altogether too short. Then James Biles said: 'Kill one of the poorest of my steers and make his hide into a rope and attach it to the one you have.' Three animals were slaughtered before a rope could be secured long enough to let the wagons down to a point where they would stand up. There one yoke of oxen was hitched to a wagon, and by locking all wheels and hitching on small logs with projecting limbs, it was taken down to a stream then known as 'Greenwater.' It took the best part of two days to make this descent. There were thirty-six wagons belonging to the company, but two of them, with a small quantity of provisions, were wrecked on this hill. The wagons could have been dispensed with without much loss. Not so the provisions, scanty as they were, as the company came to be in sore straits for food before the White River prairie was reached, probably South Prairie* of to-day, where food supplies were first obtained, consisting of potatoes without salt for the first meal. Another trying experience was the ascent of Mud Mountain in a drenching rain, with the strength of a dozen yoke of oxen attached to one wagon, with scarcely anything in it save camp equipment, and taxing the strength of the teams to the utmost. But all trials came to an end when the company reached a point six miles from Steilacoom, about October 17th, and got some good, fat beef

---

*It was Connell's Prairie. The route had been viewed at the outset through South Prairie, but afterwards it was discovered that a road had previously been opened to White River through Connell's Prairie, and the latter route was adopted and the old road cleared by Allen's party.

and plenty of potatoes, and even flour, mainly through the kindness of Dr. W. F. Tolmie. The change from salmon skins was gratifying.

"And now a word about the wagon road. That had been cut through to Greenwater. There, it seems, according to a statement made to me a number of years ago by James Longmire, and confirmed by W. O. Bush, one of the workers, an Indian from the east side of the mountains, met the road workers, who inquired of him whether there was any 'Boston men' coming through. He replied, "Wake"—no. Further inquiry satisfied the road builders that the Indian was truthful, hence they at once returned to the settlements, only to be greatly astonished two weeks later to find a weary, bedraggled, forlorn, hungry and footsore company of people of both sexes, from the babe in arms—my sister was perhaps the youngest, eleven months old, when we ceased traveling—to the man of 55 years, but all rejoicing to think that after trials indescribable they had at last reached the 'Promised Land.'

"Mrs. James Longmire says that soon after descending the big hill from the summit, perhaps early the next day, as she was a few hundred yards in advance of the teams, leading her little girl, three years and two months old. and carrying her baby boy, then fifteen months old, that she remembers meeting a man coming towards the immigrants leading a pack animal, who said to her: "Good God almighty, woman, where did you come from? Is there any more? Why, you can never get through this way. You will have to turn back. There is not a blade of grass for fifty miles."

"She replied: 'We can't go back; we've got to go forward.'

"Soon he ascended the hill by a long detour and gave supplies to the immigrants. Mrs. Longmire says she remembers hearing this man called 'Andy,' and is of the opinion that it was Andy Burge.

"When the immigrant party got to a point supposed to be about six miles from Steilacoom, or possibly near the cabin of John Lackey, it camped. Vegetables were given them by Lackey, and also by a man named Mahon. Dr. Tolmie gave a beeve. When that was sent to the camp the Doctor gave

it in charge of Mrs. Mary Ann Woolery—'Aunt Pop'—
and instructed her to keep it intact until the two oldest men
in the company came in, and that they were to divide it
evenly. Soon a man came with a knife and said he was going to have some meat. Mrs. Woolery said: 'No, sir.'
He replied: 'I am hungry, and I am going to have some of
it.' In response she said: 'So are the rest of us hungry;
but that man said I was not to allow anyone to touch it until the two oldest men came into camp, and they would divide it evenly.' He said: 'I can't wait for that.' She said:
'You will have to.' He then said: 'By what authority?'
'There is my authority,' holding up her fist—she weighed
a hundred pounds then—and she said: 'You touch that
meat and Ill take that oxbow to you,' grabbing hold of one.
The man then subsided. Soon the two oldest men came
into camp. The meat was divided according to Dr. Tolmie's directions, and, with the vegetables that had been
given, by the settlers, all hands had an old-fashioned boiled
supper—the first for many a day."

I know from experience just what such a supper meant
to that camp and how it tasted. God bless that company. I came to know nearly all of them personally,
and a bigger hearted set never lived. They earned the
right to be called Pioneers in the true sense of the word,
but a large percentage have gone on to pleasant paths,
where the remainder of us are soon to be joined in enduring fellowship.

"In the list following are the names of the Natchess Pass
immigrants of 1853. The names followed by other names
in parentheses are those of young ladies who subsequently
married men bearing the names within the parentheses:

"James Biles,* Mrs. Nancy M. Biles,* Geo. W. Biles, James
D. Biles,* Kate Biles (Sargent), Susan B. Biles (Drew),
Clark Biles,* Margaret Biles,* Ephemia Biles (Knapp), Rev.
Chas. Byles,* Mrs. Sarah W. Byles,* David F. Byles,* Mary
Jane Hill (Byles), Rebecca E. Byles (Goodell),* Chas. N.
Byles,* Sarah I. Byles (Ward), John W. Woodward,* Bar-

*Dead.

tholomew C. Baker,* Mrs. Fanny Baker,* James E. Baker,*
John W. Baker, Leander H. Baker, Elijah Baker,* Mrs.
Olive Baker,* Joseph N. Baker, Wm. LeRoy Baker, Martha
Brooks (Young),* Newton West, William R. Downey,*
Mrs. W. R. Downey,* Christopher C. Downey,* Geo. W.
Downey,* James H. Downey,* William A. Downey,* R. M.
Downey, John M. Downey, Louise Downey (Guess),* Jane
Downey (Clark)*, Susan Downey (Latham),* Laura B.
Downey (Bartlett), Mason F. Guess,* Wilson Guess,* Aus-
tin E. Young, Henry C. Finch,* Varine Davis,* James
Aiken, John Aiken, Glenn Aiken, Wesley Clinton, J. Wilson
Hampton, John Bowers, William M. Kincaid,* Mrs. W. M.
Kincaid,* Susannah Kincaid (Thompson), Joseph C. Kin-
caid, Laura Kincaid (Meade),* James Kincaid, John Kin-
caid,* James Gant, Mrs. James Gant, Harris Gant, Mrs.
Harris Gant. All the of the foregoing were from Kentucky.
Isaac Woolery,* Mrs. Isaac Woolery, Robert Lemuel Wool-
ery, James Henderson Woolery, Sarah Jane Woolery
(Ward) (born on Little Sunday), Abraham Woolery,* Mrs.
Abraham Woolery (Aunt Pop), Jacob Francis Woolery,*
Daniel Henry Woolery, Agnes Woolery (Lamon), Erastus
A. Light,* Mrs. E. A. Light,* Henry Light, George Melville,*
Mrs. George Melville,* Kate Melville (Thompson),* Robert
Melville,* Isaac H. Wright,* Mrs. I. H. Wright,* Benjamin
Franklin Wright,* Mrs. B. F. Wright, James .Wright, Eliza
Wright (Bell), Rebecca Wright (Moore), William Wright,
Byrd Wright,* Grandfather — Wright, Grandmother —
Wright, Jas. Bell, Annis Wright (Downey). The foregoing
were from Missouri. Tyrus Himes,* Mrs. Tyrus Himes,*
George H. Himes, Helen L. Himes (Ruddell), Judson W.
Himes, Lestina Z. Himes (Eaton),* Joel Risdon,* Henry
Risdon, Chas. R. Fitch,* Frederick Burnett,* James Long-
mire,* Mrs. James Longmire, Elcaine Longmire, David
Longmire, John A. Longmire, Tillathi Longmire (Kandle),
Asher Sargent,* Mrs. A. Sargent,* E. Nelson Sargent, Wil-
son Sargent,* F. M. Sargent,* Matilda Sargent (Saylor),*
Rebecca Sargent (Kellet), Van Ogle, John Lane, Mrs. John
Lane, Joseph Day, Elizabeth Whitesel (Lane), Wm.
Whitesel, Mrs. Wm. Whitesel, William Henry Whitesel.

*Dead.

Nancy Whitesel (Leach), Clark N. Greenman, Daniel E. Lane,* Mrs. D. E. Lane,* Edward Lane, William Lane, Timothy Lane, Albert Lane, Margaret Whitesel, Alexander Whitesel, Cal Whitesel. The foregoing were from Indiana. Widow Gordon, Mary Frances Gordon, or McCullough, Mrs. Mary Ann McCullough Porter, —— McCullough, —— Frazier,* Mrs. Elizabeth Frazier,* Peter Judson,* Mrs. Peter Judson,* Stephen Judson, John Paul Judson, Gertrude Shoren Judson (Delin), John Neisan.* The foregoing were from Illinois. In addition to the above were William H. Mitchell and John Stewart,* from states unknown."

This makes a total of 148 of the immigrants who completed the road—that is, all but Melville. He refused to assist in making the road and kept about a half day behind, notwithstanding James Biles asked him to lend a hand.

Accompanying the party of road workers was Quie-muth, a half-brother of Leschi, who acted as guide and led the horse upon which were packed the blankets and provisions of Parker and Allen.

---

*Dead.

CHAPTER XVIII.

Building of the Natchess Pass Road.

We have seen with what trevail the first immigrants passed through the Natchess Pass. We will now tell about that other struggle to construct any kind of a road at all, and so we must need go back a little in our story.

While I had been struggling to get the little wife and baby over from the Columbia River to the Sound, and a roof over their heads, the sturdy pioneers of this latter region set resolutely to work building a wagon road through this pass, to enable the immigration of 1853, and later years, to come direct to Puget Sound.

For unknown ages the Indians had traveled a well-worn but crooked and difficult trail through this pass, followed by the Hudson Bay people later in their intercourse with the over-mountain tribes, but it remained for the resolute pioneers of 1853 to open a wagon road over the formidable Cascade Range of mountains to connect the two sections of the new Territory, otherwise so completely separated from each other.

Congress had appropriated twenty thousand dollars for the construction of a military road from Fort Steilacoom to Wallula on the Columbia River, but it was patent to all the appropriation could not be made available in time for the incoming immigration known to be on the way.

This knowledge impelled the settlers to make extraordinary efforts to open the road, as related in this and succeeding chapters.

Meetings had been held at various points to forward the scheme and popular subscription lists circulated for prosecuting this laudable enterprise.   It was a great undertaking for the scattered pioneers, particularly where so many were newcomers with scant provision yet made for food or shelter for the coming winter.

But everyone felt this all important enterprise must be attended to, to the end that they might divert a part of the expected immigration which would otherwise go down the Columbia or through passes south of that river, and thence into Oregon, and be lost to the new but yet unorganized Territory of Washington.

And yet in the face of all the sacrifices endured and the universal public spirit manifested, there are men who would belittle the efforts of the citizens of that day and malign their memories by accusing them of stirring up discontent among the Indians. "A lot of white men who were living with Indian women, and who were interested in seeing that the country remained common pasture as long as possible." A more out- rageous libel was never penned against the living or dead.   In this case but few of the actors are left, but there are records, now fifty years old that it is a pleasure to perpetuate for the purpose of setting this matter aright, and also of correcting some errors that have crept into the treacherous memories of the living, and likewise to pay a tribute to the dead.   Later in life I knew nearly all these sixty-nine men, subscribers to this fund, and so far as I know now all are dead but eight, and I know the underlying motive that prompted this strenuous action; they wanted to see the country set- tled up with the sturdy stock of the overland immi- grants.

The same remark applies to the intrepid road workers, some of whom it will be seen camped on the trail for the whole summer, and labored without money and with- out price to the end.

It is difficult to abridge the long quotation following, illustrating so vividly as it does the rough and ready

pioneer life of Winthrop saw and so sparklingly described. Such tributes ought to be perpetuated, and I willing-
ly give up space for it from his work, "The Canoe and
Saddle," which will well repay the reader for careful
persual. Winthrop gives this account as he saw the
road-workers the last week of August, 1853, in that famous trip from Nisqually to The Dalles. Belated and a
little after nightfall, he suddenly emerged from the surrounding darkness where, quoting his words:

"A score of men were grouped about a fire. Several had
sprung up, alert at our approach. Others reposed untrou-
bled. Others tended viands odoriferous and frizzing. Others stirred the flame. Around the forest rose, black as
Erebus, and the men moved in the glare against the gloom
like pitmen in the blackest coal mines.

"I must not dally on the brink, half hid in the obscure
thicket, lest the alert ones below should suspect an ambush
and point toward me open-mouthed rifles from their stack
near at hand. I was enough out of the woods to halloo, as
I did heartily. Klale sprang forward at shout and spur.
Antipodes obeyed a comprehensible hint from the whip of
Loolowcan. We dashed down into the crimson pathway,
and across among the astonished road makers—astonished
at the sudden alighting down from Nowhere of a pair of
cavaliers, Pasaiook and Siawsh. What meant this incursion
of a strange couple? I became at once the center of a
red-flannel-shirted circle. The recumbents stood on end.
The cooks let their frying pans bubble over, while, in response to looks of expectation, I hung out my handbill and
told the society my brief and simple tale. I was not running away from any fact in my history. A harmless person, asking no favors, with plenty of pork and spongy biscuit in his bags—only going home across the continent, if
may be, and glad, gentlemen pioneers, of this unexpected
pleasure.

"My quality thus announced, the boss of the road makers,
without any dissenting voice, offered me the freedom of
their fireside. He called for the fattest pork, that I might
be entertained right republicanly. Every cook proclaimed

supper ready. I followed my representative host to the windward side of the greenwood pyre, lest smoke wafting toward my eyes should compel me to disfigure the banquet with lachrymose countenance.

"Fronting the coals, and basking in their embrowning beams, were certain diminutive targets, well known to me as defensive armor against darts of cruel hunger—cakes of unleavened bread, light flapjacks in the vernacular, confected of flour and the saline juices of fire-ripened pork, and kneaded well with drops of the living stream. Baked then in frying pan, they stood now, each nodding forward and resting its edge upon a planted twig, toasting crustily till crunching time should come. And now to every man his target!. Let supper assail us! No dastards with trencher are we.

"In such a platonic republic as this a man found his place according to his powers. The cooks were no base scullions; they were brothers, whom conscious ability, sustained by universal suffrage, had endowed with the frying pan. Each man's target of flapjacks served him for platter and edible table. Coffee, also, for beverage, the fraternal cooks set before us in infrangible tin pots—coffee ripened in its red husk by Brazilian suns thousands of leagues away, that we, in cool Northern forests, might feel the restorative power of its concentrated sunshine, feeding vitality with fresh fuel.

"But for my gramniverous steeds, gallopers all day long, unflinching steeplechase, what had nature done here in the way of provender? Alas! little or naught. This camp of plenty for me was a starvation camp for them.

"My hosts were a stalwart gang. I had truly divined them from their cleavings on the hooihut (road). It was but play for any one of these to whittle down a cedar five feet in diameter. In the morning this compact knot of comrades would explode into a mitraille of men wielding keen axes, and down would go the dumb, stolid files of the forest. Their talk was as muscular as their arms. When these laughed, as only men fresh and hearty and in the open air can laugh, the world became mainly grotesque; it seemed at once a comic thing to live—a subject for chuckling, that we were bipeds with noses—a thing to roar at; that we had all met there from the wide world to hobnob by a frolicsome fire with tin pots of coffee, and partake of crisped bacon and toasted doughboys in ridiculous abundance. Easy laughter infected the atmosphere. Echoes ceased to be pensive and became jocose. A rattling humor pervaded the feast, and Green River* rippled with noise of fantastic jollity. Civilization and its dilettante diners-out sneer when Clodpole at Dive's table doubles his soup, knifes his fish, tilts his plate into his lap, puts muscle into the crushing of his meringue, and tosses off the warm beaker in his finger bowl. Camps by Tacoma sneer not at all, but candidly roar at parallel accidents. Gawkey makes a cushion of his flapjack. Butterfingers drops his red-hot rasher into his bosom, or lets slip his mug of coffee into his boot drying by the fire—a boot henceforth saccharine. A mule, slipping his halter, steps forward unnoticed, puts his nose in the circle and brays resonant. These are the jocular boons of life, and at these the woodsmen guffaw with lusty good-nature. Coarse and rude the jokes may be, but not nasty, like the innuendoes of pseudo-refined cockneys. If the woodsmen are guilty of uncleanly wit, it differs from the uncleanly wit of cities as the mud of a road differs from the sticky slime of slums.

'It is a stout sensation to meet masculine, muscular men at the brave point of a penetrating Boston hooihut—men who are mates—men to whom technical culture means naught—men to whom myself am naught, unless I can saddle, lasso, cook, sing and chop; unless I am a man of nerve and pluck, and a brother in generosity and heartiness. It is restoration to play at cudgels of jocoseness with a circle of friendly roughs, not one of whom ever heard the word bore—with pioneers who must think and act and wrench their living from the closed hand of nature.

"* * * While fantastic flashes were leaping up and illuminating the black circuit of forest, every man made his bed, laid his blankets in starry bivouac and slept like a mummy. The camp became vocal with snores; nasal with

---

*This should read Green Water. This camp was far up in the mountains and the stream referred to came from the main range and not from the glaciers of the great mountain, and hence was a sparkling, dancing rivulet of clearest water. Green River is forty miles or more farther down the mountain.

snores of various calibre was the forest.   Some in trium-
phant tones announced that dreams of conflict and victory
were theirs; some sighed in dulcet strains that told of
lovers' dreams; some strew shrill whistles through cavern-
ous straits; some wheezed grotesquely and gasped pit-
eously; and from some who lay supine, snoring up at the
fretted roof of forest, sound gushed in spasms, leaked in
snorts, bubbled in puffs, as steam gushes, leaks and bubbles
from yawning valves in degraded steamboats.   They died
away into the music of my dreams; a few moments seemed
to pass, and it was day.

"*   *   *   If horses were breakfastless, not so were their
masters.   The road makers had insisted that I should be
their guest, partaking not only of the fire, air, earth and
water of their bivouac, but an honorable share at their
feast.   Hardly had the snoring ceased when the frying of
the fryers began.   In the pearly-gray mist of dawn, purple
shirts were seen busy about the kindling pile; in the golden
haze of sunrise cooks brandished pans over fierce coals raked
from the red-hot jaws of flame that champed their breakfast of fir logs.   Rashers, doughboys, not without molasses,
and coffee—a bill of fare identical with last night's—were
our morning meal.   *   *   *

"And so adieu, gentlemen pioneers, and thanks for your
frank, manly hospitality!   Adieu, 'Boston tilicum,' far better types of robust Americanism than some of those selected
as its representatives by Boston of the Orient, where is
too much worship of what is, and not too much uplifting of
hopeful looks of what ought to be.

"As I started, the woodsmen gave me a salute.   Down, to
echo my shout of farewell, went a fir of fifty years' standing.   It cracked sharp, like the report of a howitzer, and
crashed downward, filling the woods with shattered branch-
es.   Under cover of this first shot, I dashed at the woods.
I could ride more boldly forward into savageness, knowing
that the front ranks of my nation were following close behind."

The men who were in that camp of road workers were
E. J. Allen, A. J. Burge, Thomas Dixon, Ephraim Allen,
Jas. Henry Allen, George Githers, John Walker, John

H. Mills, R. S. More, R. Foreman, Ed. Crofts, Jas. Boise, Robert Patterson, Edward Miller, Edward Wallace, Lewis Wallace, Jas. R. Smith, John Burrow, and Jas. Mix.

The names of the workers on the east slope of the mountains are as follows: Whitfield Kirtley, Edwin Marsh, Nelson Sargent, Paul Ruddell, Edward Miller, J. W. Fonts, John L. Perkins, Isaac M. Brown, James Alverson, Nathaniel G. Stewart, William Carpenter, and Mr. Clyne.

The Pioneer and Democrat published at Olympia, in its issue of September 30th, 1854, contains the following self-explanatory letter and account that will revive the memory of many almost forgotten names and set at rest this calmuny cast upon the fame of deserving men.

"Friend Wiley: Enclosed I send you for publication the statement of the cash account of the Puget Sound emigrant road, which has been delayed until this time, partly on account of a portion of the business being unsettled, and partly because you could not, during the session of the last legislature, find room in your columns for its insertion. As you have now kindly offered, and as it is due the citizens of the Territory that they should receive a statement of the disposition of the money entrusted to me, I send it to you, and in so doing close up my connection with the Cascade road, and would respectfully express my gratitude to the citizens for the confidence they have reposed in me, and congratulate them upon the successful completion of the road.

JAMES K. HURD.

RECEIPTS.

By subscription of			John M. Swan	$ 10.00
"	"	"	S. W. Percival	5.00
"	"	"	Jos. Cushman	5.00
"	"	"	Milas Galliher	5.00
"	"	"	C. Eaton	5.00
"	"	"	Chips Ethridge	5.00
"	"	"	Wm. Berry	5.00
"	"	"	J. C. Patton	5.00
"	"	"	T. F. McElroy	5.00
"	"	"	James Taylor	5.00
"	"	"	George Gallagher	5.00
"	"	"	J. Blanchard	5.00
"	"	"	Weed & Hurd	100.00
"	"	"	Kendall Co.	50.00
"	"	"	G. A. Barnes	50.00
"	"	"	Parker, Colter & Co	30.00
"	"	"	Brand & Bettman	25.00
"	"	"	J. & C. E. Williams	25.00
"	"	"	Waterman & Goldman	25.00
"	"	"	Lightner, Rosenthal & Co	10.00
"	"	"	A. J. Moses	10.00
"	"	"	Wm. W. Plumb	10.00
"	"	"	Isaac Wood & Son	15.00
"	"	"	D. J. Chambers	20.00
"	"	"	John Chambers	5.00
"	"	"	McLain Chambers	10.00
"	"	"	J. H. Conner	5.00
"	"	"	H. G. Parsons	5.00
"	"	"	Thomas J. Chambers	20.00
"	"	"	Puget Sound Agricultural Co	100.00
"	"	"	Wells, McAllister & Co	30.00
"	"	"	Henry Murray	25.00
"	"	"	L. A. Smith	25.00
"	"	"	Chas. Wren	25.00
"	"	"	James E. Williamson	10.00
"	"	"	H. C. Mosely	5.00
"	"	"	J. M. Bachelder	5.00
"	"	"	Lemuel Bills	25.00

By subscription of W. Boatman 15.00
   "   "   " W. M. Sherwood 5.00
   "   "   " James Barron 5.00
   "   "   " S. W. Woodruff 5.00
   "   "   " R. S. More 5.00
   "   "   " John D. Press 5.00
   "   "   " Samuel McCaw 5.00
   "   "   " Philip Keach 10.00
   "   "   " Abner Martin 20.00
   "   "   " George Brail 10.00
   "   "   ' T. W. Glasgow 10.00
   "   "   " McGomery 10.00
   "   "   " Thos. Tallentire 10.00
   "   "   " Garwin Hamilton 5.00
   "   "   " John McLeod 25.00
   "   "   " Richard Philander 5.00
   "   "   " W. Gregg 5.00
   "   "   " David Pattee 20.00
   "   "   " Thomas Chambers 50.00
   "   "   " W. A. Slaughter 10.00
   "   "   " W. Hardin 15.00
   "   "   " L. Balch 50.00
   "   "   " W. W. Miller 10.00
   "   "   " J. B. Webber 25.00
   "   "   " J. W. Goodell 10.00
   "   "   " —— Kline 10.00
   "   "   " A. Benton Moses 5.00
   "   "   " —— Parsons 5.00
   "   "   " H. Hill 5.00
By amount received for horse 35.00
By amount received for horse (Woods) 35.00
By subscription of Nelson Barnes 30.00

                                                            $1,220.00
Amount note from Lemuel Bills 25.00

Whole amount received as per subscription paper......$1,195.00

This list of subscribers to the road fund will revive
memories of almost forgotten names of old-time friends

and neightbors, and also will serve to show the interest taken by all classes. It must not for a moment be taken this comprises the whole list of contributors to this enterprise, for it is not half of it, as the labor subscription far exceeded the cash receipts represented by this published statement. Unfortunately, we are unable to obtain a complete list of those who gave their time far beyond what they originally had agreed upon, but were not paid for their labor.

The *Columbian,* published under date of July 30th, 1853, says:

"Captain Lafayette Balch, the enterprising proprietor of Steilacoom, has contributed one hundred dollars in money towards the road to Walla Walla. To each and every man who started from that neighborhood to work on the road, Captain Balch gives a lot in the town of Steilacoom. He is security to the United States Government for a number of mules, pack saddles, and other articles needed by the men. He furnished the outfit for the company who started from that place with Mr. E. J. Allen, at just what the articles cost in San Francisco."

Mr. Hurd's expenditure is set out in his published report, but none of it is for labor, except for Indian hire, a small sum. We know there were thirty men at work at one time, and that at least twelve of them spent most of the summer on the work and that at least fifty laborers in all donated their time, and that the value of the labor was far in excess of the cash outlay.

By scanning the list the "Old Timer" will readily see the cash subscribers and road workers were by no means confined to Olympia, and that many of the old settlers of Pierce County are represented, and even the foreign corporation, the Puget Sound Agricultural Company, came down with a heavy subscription. Everybody was in favor of the road. Such can also pick out the names of those "white men who were living with

Indian women" among the liberal subscribers to the fund for opening the road.

Nor were the Indians lacking in interest in the enterprise. A. J. Baldwin, then and for many years afterwards a citizen of Olympia, and whom it may be said was known as a truthful man, in a recent interview, said:

"We all put our shoulders to the wheel to make the thing go. I helped to pack out grub to the working party myself. It seemed to be difficult to get the stuff out; entirely more so than to get it contributed. I was short of pack animals one trip, and got twelve horses from Leschi, and I believe Leschi went himself also."*

" 'Do you remember how much you paid Leschi for his horses?'

" 'Why, nothing. He said if the whites were working without pay and were giving provisions, it was as little as he could do to let his horses go and help. He said if I was giving my time and use of horses then he would do the same, and if I received pay then he wanted the same pay I got. Neither of us received anything.' "

These were the Indians, as the reader will see by perusal of later chapters, who were actually driven from their farms into the war camp, leaving the plow and unfinished furrow in the field and stock running at large, to be confiscated by the volunteers.

And such were the road workers in the Natchess Pass in the fall of 1853, and such were the pioneers of that day. Fortunate it is we have the testimony of such a gifed and unbiased writer as Winthrop to delineate the character of the sturdy men who gave their strenuous efforts and substance that their chosen commonwealth might prosper.

---

*Baldwin is mistaken. Queimuth, Leschi's brother, went as guide and packer, but Leschi doubtless supplied the horses.

CHAPTER XIX.

Building the Natchess Pass Road—Concluded.

Allen's party left Steilacoom for this work July 30th, (1853), and was still at work on the 26th of September, when he wrote: "We will be through this week, having completed the western portion of the road." With twenty men in sixty days and over sixty miles to cut, he could not be expected to build much of a road.

The other party, under Kirtley, left Olympia, thirteen strong, July 19th, and was back again August 20th, and so could not have done very effective work on the east slope, as it would take at least a third of the time to make the trip out and back from their field of labor.

With the view of trying to settle the disputed points, I wrote to my old time friend, A. J. Burge, one of the Allen party, to get information from first hands, and have this characteristic reply:

"Wenass, December 8th, 1904.

"Friend Meeker.—Sir: Your letter dated Nov. 26, 1904, at hand. Sir, I am quite sick. I will try to sit up long enough to scratch an answer to your questions. Kirtley's men fell out among themselves. I well remember Jack Perkins had a black eye. Kirtley, as I understood, was to go (to) Wenass creek, thence cut a wagon road from Wenass to the Natchess River, thence up the Natchess River until they met Allen's party. It is my opinion they did commence at Wenass. There were three notches cut in many of the large trees (logs). I can find some of these trees yet where these notches show. Allen did not know Kirtley and his party had abandoned the enterprise until Ehformer told him. He expressed much surprise and re-

gret. I packed the provisions for Allen's party. The last
trip I made I found Allen and his party six or eight miles
down the Natchess River. I was sent back to the summit
of the mountain to search for a pack mule and a pack horse.
These two animals were used by the working party to move
their camp outfit, and their provisions. When they returned
they told me that they cut the road down to where Kirtley's
party left off. Of my own knowledge I can safely say Allen's party cut the road from John Montgomery's* to some
six or maybe eight miles down the Natchess River, and it
was four days after that before they came to the summit on
their return.

"It is possible Kirtley's party slighted their work to the
extent that made it necessary for the immigrants to take
their axes in hand. I consider Kirtley a dead failure at anything. Kirtley's party came home more than a month before
we came in. If Van Ogle is not insane he ought to remember.

"Allen's party cut the road out from six to eight miles
down the Natchess River to John Montgomery's. The valley
on the Natchess River is too narrow for any mistake to
occur.

"The first men that came through came with James and
his brother, Charles Biles, Sargent, Downey, James Longmire, Van Ogle, two Atkins, Lane, a brother-in-law of Sargent, Kincaid, two Woolery's, Lane of Puyallup, E. A.
Light, John Eagan (Reagan), Charley Fitch. Meeker, I
am quite sick; when I get well I will write more detailed
account; it is as much as I can do to sit up.

"Yours in haste, as ever,

"A. J. BURGE."

This man I have known for over fifty years, and it
touched me to think at the age bordering on eighty, he
should get up out of a sick bed to comply with my request. He has written the truth, and some of the information we could get in no other way.

*Nisqually Plains.

It seems that some people live a charmed life. Burge was shot by a would-be assassin a few miles out from Steilacoom over forty years ago, the bullet going through his neck, just missing the jugular vein.

While it is a complete digression, nevertheless, just as interesting here as elsewhere, so I will tell the story of this shooting to further illustrate conditions of early settlement on the Nisqually plains. The man with the thirteen cows and thirty calves mentioned elsewhere, lived near Burge. The most desperate character I ever knew, Charles McDaniel, also was a near neighbor, but a friend of Andy, as we used to call Burge. Both lost stock that could be traced directly to their neighbor, Wren, the man with the extra calves, but it was no use to prosecute him as a jury could not be procured that would convict. I had myself tried it in our court with the direct evidence of the branded hide taken from him, but a bribed juryman refused to convict. For a few years and for this district and with the class previously described as occupying the country adjacent to Steilacoom, there seemed to be no redress through our courts. Finally Burge and McDaniel waylaid their neighbor a few miles out from Steilacoom, tied him to a tree, and whipped him most unmercifully. I have never yet given my approval to mob law and never will, believing that it is better to suffer awhile, bide one's time until laws can be enforced, rather than to join in actions that will breed contempt for law and lead to anarchy. But, if ever there was a justifiable case of men taking the law in their own hands, this was one of them, and is introduced here to illustrate a condition of affairs that had grown up which seemed well nigh intolerable. After the whipping Wren was warned to leave the country, which he could not well do, tied to a tree as he was until third parties discovered and released him, but which he speedily did, although the wealthiest man in the county. No prosecutions followed, but in the lapse of

time a colored man appeared at Steilacoom and spent
much time hunting herds on the prairies, until one day
Burge was going home from Steilacoom in his wagon,
when this centre shot was fired with the result as related. The colored man disappeared as mysteriously as
he came, but everyone believed he had been hired to
assassinate Burge and McDaniel, and as afterwards
proven was the case.

But the trouble was not ended here. The lawless
neighbor had gone, but not lawlessness. The old story
that lawlessness begets lawlessness was again proven.
McDaniel and others concluded that as Wren was gone,
they could prey upon his land holdings, which for twen-
ty-five years in Pierce County was no more than squatter's rights, in consequence of that intolerable claim of
the Puget Sound Agricultural Company, mentioned
elsewhere. At this, most of the community rebelled and
warned McDaniel, but to no purpose, until finally he was
shot down on the streets of Steilacoom, or rather a
vacant lot in a public place, and lay for hours in his
death struggles uncared for, and his pal murdered in
the wagon that was carrying him to a scaffold. The
two had been waylaid, but had escaped, only to meet
their fate in a more public manner. Burge narrowly
escaped a like fate at the hands of the mob, because of
his near neighborship with McDaniel and of his
participation with him in the first instance that had
led up to the final catastrophe. But Burge was an honorable man, though rough in manner, yet just in his
dealings, while McDaniel was a gambler and a black-
leg of the very worst, imaginable type. The Indian war
had brought to the front many vicious characters, and
the actions of some officials in high places had encouraged lawlessness, so, as a community, the near by country round and about Steilacoom was scourged almost
beyond belief.

And yet there were genuine pioneer settlements in

not very far off regions of this storm center of lawlessness, where the law was as cheerfully obeyed as in any
old and well settled community, where crime was scarcely known, and where family ties were held as sacred as
any place on earth, and where finally the influence
spread over the whole land and the whole community
leavened.

By these incidents related it will be seen that pioneers
were neither all saints nor all sinners, but like with older
communities had their trials other than the supposed
discomforts incident to pioneer life.

The reader may not have noticed that Burge in his
letter mentions that there are still trees (he means
logs), yet to be seen with the three notches cut in them,
where the immigrant road had been cut. I had forgotten the third notch, but it all comes back to me now
that he has mentioned it. These logs that we bridged
up to and cut the notches in for the wheels in most
cases had to have the third notch in the center to save
the coupling pole or reach from catching on the log,
especially where the bridging did not extend out far
from the log to be crossed. Oftentimes the wagon would
be unloaded, the wagon box taken off, the wagon un-
coupled and taken over the obstruction or down or up
it, as the case might be, to be loaded again beyond.

It will be noticed by Mr. Himes' letter that their party
came all the way up the canyon and crossed the Natchess
River 68 times while I crossed it but thirty odd times.
At or near the 32d crossing, the road workers took to
the table land and abandoned the lower stretch of the
canyon, and through that portion the train which Mr.
Himes refers to was compelled to cut their own road for
a long stretch. But that part reported cut was certainly a hard road to travel, and we had to work more
or less all the way down the mountain; as Colonel E.
J. Allen, who is yet alive, quaintly put it in a recent
letter: "Assuredly the road was not sand papered." I

should say not. I think the Colonel was not much of a teamster and had never handled the goad stick over the road or elsewhere, as I did, else he would be more sympathetic in responses to outcries against the "execrable shadow of a road."

Nelson Sargent mentioned by Mr. Himes still lives and is a respected, truthful citizen, but he certainly did take great risks in leading that first train of immigrants into that trap of an uncut road up the Natchess River. The whole party narrowly escaped starvation in the mountains and Sargent a greater risk of his neck at the hands of indignant immigrants while in the mountains, if we may believe the reports that came out at the time from the rescued train. However, I never believed that Sargent intended to deceive, but was oversanguine and was himself deceived, and that Kirtley's failure to continue in the field was the cause of the suffering that followed.

Allen sent 300 pound of flour to Wenas and a courier came out to Olympia, whereupon "Old Mike Simmons," Bush, Jones, and others, forthwith started with half a ton of flour, onions, potatoes, etc., and met them beyond the outskirts of the settlement. All that was necessary those days for a person to get help was to let it become known that some one was in distress and there would always be willing hands without delay; in fact, conditions almost approached the socialistic order of common property as to food, by the voluntary actions of the great, big hearted early settlers, as shown in other instances related, as well as in this. God bless those early settlers, the real pioneers of that day.

The Indian Leschi, who we have seen contributed to the work, utilized the road to make his escape with seventy of his people, after his disastrous defeat at the hands of the volunteers and United States troops in March, 1856, to cross the summit on the snow, so that after all, in a way, he received a benefit from his liberality in times of peace.

Two years after the opening the road, the Hudson Bay Company sent a train of three hundred horses loaded with furs, from the interior country to Fort Nisqually, with a return of merchandise through the same pass, but never repeated the experiment.

CHAPTER XX.

The Mud Wagon Road.

Writing of the Natchess Pass immigrant road reminds me of another that everybody said was "a bad road," and most people, that "it is the worst road I ever saw in all my life." I refer to the old road from Monticello, on the Cowlitz River, near the Columbia River, to Olympia.

Monticello was more a name than a town, being the farm house and outbuildings of Uncle Darb Huntington, as we all called him, with a blacksmith shop, store, two or three families and a stable. Here the passengers were dumped from the little steamers from Portland and other Columbia River points, and here, in the earliest days, the hapless traveler either struck the trail (afterwards supplanted by the road), or would tuck himself with others into a canoe, like sardines in a box, where an all-day journey was his fate, unmoved and immovable except as an integral part of the frail craft that carried him to "Hard Breads" tavern for the night. We have taken a peep into Hard Bread's hostelry in a previous chapter, and of the trail and canoe passage, but that was before the days of the road now under notice. At first, travelers to the Sound ascended the Cowlitz to the landing farther up the river than where the mud-wagon road left the Cowlitz, and from the landing were sent on their way by saddle train or over the make-shift of a road cut by the Simmons-Bush party in 1845, over which they dragged their effects on sleds to the head of the Sound, or, to be specific, to the mouth of the Deschutes River, afterwards and now known as Tumwater.

I have no history of the construction of the later road

all the way up the right bank of the Cowlitz to the mouth of the Toutle River (Hard-Breads'), and thence deflecting northerly to the Chehalis, where the old and new routes were joined, and soon emerged into the gravelly prairies, where there were natural road beds everywhere. The facts are, this road, like Topsy, "just growed," and so gradually became a highway one could scarcely say when the trail ceased to be simply a trail and the road actually could be called a road. First, only saddle trains could pass. On the back of a stiff jointed, hard trotting, slow walking, contrary mule, I was initiated into the secret depths of the mud holes of this trail. And such mud holes! It became a standing joke after the road was opened that a team would stall with an empty wagon going down hill, and I came very near having just such an experience once, within what is now the city limits of the thriving city of Chehalis.

After the saddle train came the mud wagons in which passengers were conveyed (or invited to walk over bad places, or preferred to walk), over either the roughest corduroy or deepest mud, the one bruising the muscles the other straining the nerves in the anticipation of being dumped into the bottomless pit of mud.

In 1853, Henry Winsor ran canoes up the Cowlitz River to what was known as Cowlitz Landing, where Fred A. Clark kept a hotel, and also horses for a saddle train to Olympia. Clark afterwards became my neighbor in the Puyallup Valley, and Winsor lived for many years in Olympia, and now lives near Shelton, Mason County, in this state, at the ripe age of nearly eighty years.

Following the change of route Winsor transferred his interests from the water route to the land, and extended his field to the Sound, and finally, as related, became a resident of Olympia.

This reminds me of Winsor's marriage to Miss Huntington, daughter of "Uncle Darb," under circumstances so peculiar that I am again tempted to digress and tell about the wedding. Because of the prominence of the parties, and peculiar circumstances attending it, the wedding had been the talk of the day from one end of the land to the other.

The illustration on the opposite page shows these pioneer, fifty years after, what a friend terms "their romantic and unique wedding" at Rainier, June 2d, 1853.

Reluctantly Mrs. Winsor has supplied the facts that led to the marriage without courtship, and to a life of pleasant paths of honorable citizenship.

"At that time any one wishing the service of a minister," she writes, "had to send to Portland. Rev. C. H. Kingsley had been down to Rainier to marry a couple just two weeks before. Mr. Winsor was one of the guests, and also one at the marriage of Mr. Fox and Miss Dray, and as everyone was joking him unmercifully about losing Miss Dray, he was wearing crape on his hat, but did not act like he was mourning much. Quite a crowd went from Monticello. There was lots of fun. There were Miss Burbee and Mr. Smith (married later), Mr. Winsor and Miss Chapman, Charles Holman (afterwards Captain Holman on Columbia River boats for many years), and myself and others.

"I was young and thoughtless—anything for fun. Girls were scarce in those days and took many privileges. Two or three young men were there and they were teasing me, and I suppose I was a little saucy. As we were at supper Mr. Winsor said to Mr. Kingsley: 'You better marry a lot of them this time so you won't have to come so often.' He said, 'Here is Mr. Smith and Miss Burbee, Mr. Holman and Miss Huntington, and so on.' The first said they were not ready. Mr. H. said he would have to wait till he asked her father. Mr. Winsor then turned to me and asked if I was ready. I asked him if he ever knew a girl that was not ready to marry, if she had a chance, and so one thing led to another, and finally Mr. Kingsley proposed that, as we seemed the only ones ready, we had better be married, and

MR. AND MRS. HENRY WINSOR

Mr. Winsor then said he guessed we would have to wait till he could see my father, and I then supposed that ended it, but every now and then something else would come up, and they finally dared us to sit down in the chairs that the couple had just occupied (the supper was before the ceremony there), and we did so. Then they dared us to stand up. Some of them told the minister to say the ceremony in fun. He said: 'If I say the ceremony it will be no fun.' We did not know he said that. There did not have to be a license then. We still stood. Then the minister came forward. We thought he would say a long ceremony, as he did before, and Mr. Winsor thought if I didn't back out he would, but I think he meant to punish us for our frivolity, and said a very short ceremony and pronounced us man and wife before we had time to think. It was such a shock that Mr. Winsor could not speak when he realized what we had done. I was so much younger and full of Old Nick that I did not realize it as soon as he did. I went home to my father's house and stayed about two weeks. Mr. Winsor was visiting me there. He said as we neither of us cared for another that if I was willing and wished it, as we had been so foolish, we would try what life had in store for us together. We celebrated our fiftieth anniversary last June."

This frank letter was written upon the author's earnest solicitation to "get at the truth of the matter," and the lady wrote privately because there had been so much misrepresentation published, she complied with the request. The aged couple still live in Mason County not far from Olympia.

I have already told of my trip from the Columbia River to the Sound by the trail and wagon road. Subsequently the trial of a mule back ride, to be followed later in the mud wagon, and after that the stage coach, all of these modes of travel it had fallen my lot to test. When the rail road came in 1873, it was my good fortune to make the trip in the first car that ran out from Tacoma carrying passengers, of which there were five of us, including General John W. Sprague, the superintendent of the road.

CHAPTER XXI.

The Fraser River Stampede.

On the 21st day of March, 1858, the Schooner Wild Pigeon arrived at Steilacoom, and brought the news that the Indians had discovered gold on Fraser River; had traded several pounds of the precious metal with the Hudson Bay Company, and that three hundred people had left Victoria and vicinity for the new eldorado. And further, the report ran the mines were exceedingly rich.

The next day there came further reports from the north, that the Bellingham Bay Company's coal mines had been compelled to suspend work, as all their operatives but three had started for the mines, that many of the logging camps had shut down, and all the mills were running on short time from the same cause.

The wave of excitement that ran through the little town upon the receipt of this news was repeated in every town and hamlet of the whole Pacific Coast, and continued around the world, sending thither adventurous spirits from all civilized countries of the earth.

But when the word came the next week that one hundred and ten pounds of gold had actually been received in Victoria, and that hundreds of men were outfitting, the virulence of the gold fever knew no bounds, and everybody, women folks and all, wanted to go, and would have started pell-mell had there not been that restraining influence of the second sober thought of people who had just gone through the mill of adversity. My family was still in the block house we had built during the war in the town of Steilacoom. Our cattle were peacefully grazing on the plains a few miles distant, but there remained a spirit of unrest that one could not fail to observe. There had been no Indian depredations for two years west of the Cascade Mountains, but some atrocious murders had been committed by a few renegade white men, besides the murder of Leschi under the forms of law that had but recently taken place. The Indians just over the mountains were in a threatening mood, and in fact soon again broke out into open warfare and inflicted heavy punishment on Steptoe's command, and came very near annihilating that whole detachment.

The close of the Indian war of 1855-6 had engendered a reckless spirit among what may be called the unsettled class that to many of the more sober minded was looked upon as more dangerous than the Indians among us. In the wake of the United States army paymaster came a vile set of gamblers and blacklegs that preyed upon the soldiers, officers and men alike, who became a menace to the peace of the community, and, like a veritable bedlam turned loose, often made night hideous with their carousals. The reader need not feel this is an overdrawn picture for it is not. We must remember the common soldiers of the United States army fifty years ago were very different from our army of the present time. At least such was the case with the forces stationed at Fort Steilacoom at the time of which I am writing.

One illustration. Having drifted into a small business conducted in our block house at Steilacoom, in an unguarded moment I let a half dozen of the blue-coats (as the soldiers were then universally called), have a few articles on credit. These men told their comrades, who came soliciting credit but were refused, when some drunken members of the party swore they would come strong enough to take the goods anyway, and actually did come at night thirty strong, and having been refused admission, began breaking down the door. A shot

through the door that scattered splinters among the
assembled crowd served as a warning that caused them
to desist, and no damage was done, but the incident
serves to illustrate the conditions prevailing at the
time the gold discovery was reported. Pierce County
contributed its contingent of gold seekers, some of the
desperados and some of the best citizens. One Charles
McDaniel, who killed his man while gone returned to
plague us; another, one of our merchants, Samuel Mc-
Caw, bundled up a few goods, made a flying trip up
Fraser River, came back with fifty ounces of gold dust
and with the news the mines were all that had been reported, and more too, which of course added fuel to the
burning flame of the all-prevalent gold fever. We all
then believed a new era had dawned upon us, similar to
that of ten years before in California that changed the
world's history. High hopes were built, most of them
to end in disappointment. Not but there were extensive
mines, and that they were rich, and that they were
easily worked, but, how to get there was the puzzling
question. The early voyagers had slipped up the Fraser
before the freshets that came from the melting snows
to swell the torrents of that river. Those going later
either failed altogether and gave up the unequal contest,
or lost an average of one canoe or boat out of three
in the persistent attempt. How many lives were lost,
never will be known.

"Beginning at a stump in the bank of said creek
(Squalecum), about 20 feet above the bridge near the
mouth of said creek; thence running due west 240 feet;
thence due south 60 feet; thence due east 240 feet;
thence due north 60 feet to the place of beginning."
Such is the description of a tract of land as recorded
on the book of records of deeds for the county of Whatcom, bearing date of June 25th, 1858. On that date
I was in Whatcom, and saw the sights and acted my part
as one of the wild men of the north country, received

a deed for the land as described from Edward Eldridge, who then resided on his claim adjoining the town of Whatcom, and where he continued until his death. No public surveys had up to that time been made, and so, to describe a lot I was purchasing of Mr. Eldridge, what more durable monument could we select than a big stump of one of those giants of the monster forests fronting on Bellingham Bay.

Going back a little in my story to the receipt of the news of the discovery on the Fraser and Thompson Rivers, each succeeding installment of news that came to Steilacoom more than confirmed the original report. Contingents began to arrive in Steilacoom from Oregon, from California, and finally from "the States," as all of our country east of the Rocky Mountains was designated by pioneers. Steamers great and small began to appear with more or less cargo and passenger lists, which we heard were as nothing compared to what was going on less than a hundred miles to the north of us. These people landing in Whatcom in such great numbers must be fed, we agreed, and if the multitude would not come to us to drink the milk of our dairies and eat the butter, what better could we do than to take our cows to the multitude where we were told people did not hesitate to pay a dollar a gallon for milk and any price one might ask for fresh butter.

But, how to get even to Whatcom was the "rub." All space on the steamers was taken from week to week for freight and passengers, and no room left for cattle. In fact, the movement of provisions was so great that at one time we were almost threatened with a veritable famine, so close had the stock of food been shipped. Finally, our cattle, mostly cows, were loaded in an open scow and taken in tow along side of the steamer (Sea Bird, I think it was), where all went smoothly enough until we arrived off the head of Whidby Island, where a chopped sea from a light wind began slopping over

into the scow and evidently would sink us despite our
utmost efforts at bailing. When the captain would slow
down the speed of his steamer all was well, but the
moment greater power was applied, over the gunwales
would come the water. The dialogue that ensued between myself and the Captain was more emphatic than
elegant and perhaps would not look well in print, but
he dare not either let go of us or run us under without
incurring the risk of heavy damages and probable loss
of life. But I stood by my guns (figuratively), and
would not consent to be landed, and so about the 20th
of June, tired and sleepy, we were set adrift in Bellingham Bay, and landed near the big stump described
as the starting point for the land purchased later.

But our cows must have feed, must be milked, and
the milk marketed, and so there was no rest nor sleep
for us for another thirty-six hours. In fact, there was
but little sleep for anybody on that beach at the time.
Several ocean steamers had just dumped three thousand
people on the beach, and the scramble still continued
to find a place to build a house or stretch a tent, or
even to spread a blanket, for there were great numbers
already on hand landed by previous steamers. The
staking of lots on the tide flats at night, when the tide
was out, seemed to be a staple industry. Driving of
piles or planting of posts as permanent as possible often
preceded and accompanied by high words between con-
testants came to be a commonplace occurrence. The
belief among these people seemed to be that if they
could get stakes or posts to stand on end, and a six-
inch strip nailed to them to encompass a given spot of
the flats, that they would thereby become the owner,
and so the merry war went on until the bubble bursted.

A few days after my arrival four steamers came with
an aggregate of over two thousand passengers, many of
whom, however, did not leave the steamer and took passage either to their port of departure San Francisco,

Victoria, or points on the Sound. The ebb tide had set in, and although many steamers came later and landed passengers, their return lists soon became large and the population began to diminish.

Taking my little dory that we had with us on the scow, I rowed out to the largest steamer lying at anchor surrounded by small boats so numerous that in common parlance the number was measured by the acre, "an acre of boats." Whether or not an acre of space was covered by these crafts striving to reach the steamer I will not pretend to say, but can say that I certainly could not get within a hundred feet of the steamer. All sorts of craft filled the intervening space, from the smallest Indian canoe to large barges, the owners of each either striving to secure a customer from a hapless passenger, or, having secured one, of transferring his belongings to the craft.

There were but a few women in this crowd, but ashore, quite too many, a large majority of whom (those on the ground will remember), were too much like their arch representative, "Old Mother Damnable," well and truly named. But I draw the veil.

"Where's DeLacy?" became a by-word after weeks of earnest inquiry of the uninitiated as to what was transpiring out at the front, where supposed work was going on to construct a trail leading through the Cascade Mountains to the mouth of Thompson River, that emptied into the Fraser one hundred and fifty miles easterly from Whatcom. If a trail could be constructed through the mountains from Whatcom, then the town would at once bloom into a city, and the fortunes of townsite proprietors would be made, and all might go to the mines whose spirit moved them. It all looked very feasible on paper, but several obstacles not taken into account by the impatient crowd defeated all their hopes. A fund had been raised by subscription at the inception of the excitement to send out parties to search for a pass, and W. W. DeLacy, an engineer of considerable note, started out early in the season, and so far as I know never came back to Whatcom.

Directly this party was sent out to search for a pass through the mountains another party was set to work to follow and cut the trail. All seemingly went well for awhile, and until there came no word to the public from DeLacy. The trail workers were yet at work, but did not know what was ahead of them. DeLacy had to them become a sort of myth. The fact was he had failed to find a pass, and when he arrived at a point that he thought was the summit, he had yet fifty miles or more of the worst of the mountains ahead of him. Meanwhile, the trail out from Whatcom for forty or fifty miles became well worn by men and animals going and returning. I saw sixty men with heavy packs on their backs start out in one company, everyone of whom had to come back after floundering in the mountains for weeks. So long as there could be kept up a hope that the trail would be cut through, just so long a complete collapse of the townsite boom might be averted, and so DeLacy was kept in the mountains searching for a pass which was never found.

About the time I landed in Whatcom, H. L. Yesler and Arthur A. Denny headed a party to go through the Snoqualmie Pass, but they did not reach the open country. W. H. Pearson, the intrepid scout, who won such laurels with Governor Stevens in his famous ride from the Blackfeet country, conducted a party of eighty-two persons, sixty-seven of whom packed their bedding and food on their backs, through the Snoqualmie Pass to the Wenatchee, where they were met by the Indians in such numbers and threatening mood that nearly all beat a hasty retreat.

Simultaneous with the movement through the Snoqualmie Pass, like action was set on foot to utilize the Natchess Pass, and large numbers must have gotten

through as on August 7th the report was published
that fourteen hundred miners were at work on the Natchess and Wenatchee. This report we known to be un-
true, although it is possible that that many prospectors
were on those rivers, and we know also some gold was
taken out, and more for many years afterwards. But the
mines on these rivers did not prove to be rich nor extensive.

At the same time efforts were made to reach the mines
by crossing the mountains further south. The people
of Oregon were sure the best way was to go up the
Columbia River to The Dalles, and thence north through
the open country, and more than a thousand men were
congregated at The Dalles at one time preparing to make
the trip northward.

All this while the authorities of British Columbia
were not asleep, but fully awake to their own interests.
Soon Governor Dougless put a quietus upon parties
going direct from Puget Sound ports into the Fraser
River, and several outfits of merchandise were confiscated, among which was one of McCaw and Rogers from
Steilacoom. Another effectual barrier was the prohibi-
tion from entering the country without a miner's license,
which could be obtained only at Victoria. In this way
the Whatcom game was blocked, with or without a trail,
and the population disappeared nearly as rapidly and
more mysteriously than it had come, and the houses that
had been built were left tenantless, the stakes that had
been set were left to be swept away by the tides or to
decay, and Whatcom for a time became only a memory
to its once great population.

It is doubtful if a stampede of such dimensions ever
occurred where the suffering was so great, the prizes so
few and the loss of life, proportionately greater than that
to the Fraser in 1858. Probably not one in ten that
made the effort reached the mines, and of those who
did the usual percentage of blanks was drawn incident

to such stampedes. And yet, the mines were immensely rich, and many millions of dollars of gold value came from the find in the lapse of years, and is still coming, though now nearly fifty years has passed.

While the losses to the people of the Puget Sound country were great, nevertheless, good came out of the great stampede in the large accession of population that stayed after the return tide was over. Many had become stranded and could not leave the country, but went to work wth a will, of whom not a few are still honored citizens of the State that has been carved out of the Territory of that day.

AN OLD SETTLERS' MEETING

CHAPTER XXII.

An Old Settlers' Meeting.

The fact that the generation that participated in the Indian war in this State (then Territory) will soon pass, an attempt was made to hold a reunion of all the adults who were in Pierce County at the outbreak of the Indian war in 1855, who are still living in the county.

Naturally, the incidents of the war coming under personal observation formed a never-ending topic of conversation. Mrs. Boatman related the incident of her boy "Johnny" (John Boatman, who now lives in Puyallup), two years and a half old, who was carried off by the Indians, as she firmly believes, but was found under an oak tree the following day. The whole garrison at Steilacoom turned out, together with a great many citizens, and scoured the prairie all night. Colonel Casey, the commandant, threatened vengeance against the Indians if the child was not returned. The theory was that the Indians had taken him for a ransom of their own people held by the whites.

A romantic incident was recalled of Kate Melville, the lady deputy sheriff. Her father was the first sheriff of Pierce County, and during his term of office was imprisoned for contempt of court. Kate was a beautiful girl, in ideal health, and a superb equestrian, but withal was a modest, retiring woman. When her father was incarcerated she was aroused to action and accepted the appointment of deputy sheriff with a resolute spirit, determined to take the responsibility of enforcing the law.

"Yes, I saw Kate coming down from the garrison one

day with some prisoners with a pistol strapped to her person," said Willis Boatman, "but I do not remember what her father was imprisoned for."

Scarcely one present but rememberd the incident "that seemed like a dream almost," in the lapse of forty-five years.

I remember seeing Kate on horseback, while acting as deputy sheriff during those troublous times, and had often thought to write up this romantic incident of stern real pioneer life, but space will not permit it here, further than to say that the responsibilities of the office were undertaken from a sense of duty and under intense loyalty to her father. Both now lie peacefully under the sod in the county in which their lot was cast.

"We moved out to my father's place about two months after the outbreak of the war," said George Dougherty. "The Indians sent us word not to be afraid—that they would not harm us. I had lived among the Indians from childhood, and in fact had learned to talk the Indian language before I could speak my mother tongue. At that time I believe there were twenty Indians to where there is one now. Most of the Indians were friendly. Had it been otherwise they could have wiped out the white settlement completely, in spite of the military and volunteers."

"Yes, and not left a grease spot of them," said Mr. Rogers. "But the fact is, the Indians did not want to fight the whites, but were dissatisfied with their treatment by the government. They wanted their land back, and got it, too, after they whipped the whites, which they did this side of the mountains. If it had not been that a majority of the Indians were in favor of peace with the whites, they could have held this country for a number of years. In fact, there were fifty or sixty Indians who fought on the side of the whites. There were a lot of whites who intended to stay out on their ranches, as they had perfect confidence in the Indians. The result of the war was that the Indians got all that they contended for. The good bottom land had been taken away from the Indians and they had been given the woods. This was done to open up the bottom lands for settlement. Notwithstanding this, many of the Indians were not hostile enough to go to war. The Indians east of the mountains initiated the war when they came over here and insisted that these Indians drive out the whites. In the meantime the Indians were given their lands back again. The Indians killed as many whites as the whites killed Indians. They had been living at peace with the whites and would have continued to do so had it not been for the Indians east of the mountains. I think that a mean advantage of the Indians was taken at that treaty."

"I think there were as many whites killed this side of the mountains as Indians," said Mr. Dougherty, resuming; "and there would have been no war had the Indians been properly treated. I remember Leschi and his band passed down through the prairie near my father's house, but did not stop to disturb us, but moved on to Muckleshoot and Green River."

"Yes, I remember considerable about the early condition of the Indian and their supply of food, for many and many is the time that I have enjoyed their hospitality and partaken of the various forms of what may be termed their land food as distinguished from fish. This was varied and abundant. I have seen trainloads of dried camas and sunflower roots carried by their ponies, and sometimes by the squaws on their backs. The Indians called the sunflower roots 'kalse.' It has now become almost extinct, except in small fields where it is protected. Kalse is a small root, about the size of an ordinary carrot, and has a yellow flower resembling the sunflower. The Indians would dig it with a crooked staff of ironwood stick, by twisting the stick among the roots and using it as a lever to pull up the roots. After getting a sufficient quantity of this sunflower root together the tops of the roots would be nipped off, then the bark would be beaten off and a baking place arranged in a hollow in the ground, with sallal berry twigs, leaves and hemlock boughs. The roots would be piled up rounding, and covered over with the sallal and other material, and the whole covered with earth. A fire would be made over the ground and the roasting would occupy three or four days, depending upon the size of the pile. After the end of three or four days the remaining coals and hot ashes would be removed from the top of the pile, and there would be exposed the steaming sunflower roots. The roots are very delicious in taste, though I cannot compare it to anything now in use. They also made a liquor from its roots by soaking, which was very exhilarating and strengthening. I have often partaken of this food when a child. There was another food gathered from the prairie, which the Indians called 'lacamas' or 'camas.' It is a small root, about the size of the end of your thumb, and has a stalk that shows itself early in the spring. It comes up as two leaves folded together, and as it progresses in growth it spreads. From this appears a stem on the top of which is a blue flower. It is very nutritious. It was generally prepared in large quantities and could be kept until the following year. I have always thought that it would be a great addition to our garden products, and would be beneficial to us as a health diet generally. The Indians who used it were generally very healthy. There is another article of food that I know the Indian name for, but not the white man's. The Indian name is 'squelebs.' It grows in low, marshy places and in creeks that run cold, clear water. It has the appearance of the wild parsnip, and probably is a species of it. It grows in joints. It is very delicious to the taste in its season and is eaten raw. It is the finest nervine that I ever used. Then comes 'kinnikinneck' berries, or the Indian tobacco. The Indians will take 'kinnikinnick' leaves, roast them until brown, and then mix half and half with tobacco, when it makes very fine smoking, and the odor is fragrant and very acceptable. It has an influence over the smoker like opium or ether. Some Indians that I have seen using it would keel over in a trance. It is very highly prized by them. The berries that grow and ripen on the 'kinnikinnick' when ripe are used as food by the Indians by mixing them with dried salmon eggs, and have the property of strengthening to an abnormal degree. They also used the young sprouts of the wild raspberry and salmon berry, which were very useful in cooling the system and very acceptable to the palate. There was another food product that the Indians called 'charlaque.' It throws out a broad, dark green leaf on one side of the stem, and on the end of the stem there is a bell-shaped flower of a brownish cast on the outside, and on the inside the color is orange, mottled with brown specks. It produces a flat root about the size of an ordinary walnut and is good either raw or roasted. It grows in shady places and near oak bushes. The root is white. There is also a species of the dandelion which has a very delicate-tasting root, which was eaten either raw or roasted. It is something similar to the wild parsnip, and the root is also white. When the root is broken it exudes a milk which is an excellent cure for warts. Another food plant was the 'wapato.' It grows in swampy places and sends its roots into the water. It grows luxuriantly in such places, and the tubers of the 'wapata' were highly prized by the Indians and could be eaten either raw or cooked. It had a delicate and pungent taste that was very acceptable to the palate. By this you will see that the Indians had a variety of food, when one takes into consideration the wild fruits, fish and game in which the country abounded."

Peter Smith* said: "We were crossing the plains in 1852 when Spotted Tail with about thirty warriors, fresh from the Crow war, rode up to our camp early one

*Died recently.

morning. I was cooking breakfast for our party, and I tell you I was pretty well scared, but I thought to offer them something to eat and after several attempts made them understand what I wanted, and finally gave them all a breakfast of bread and sugar and coffee. When they first came they sat on their horses with feathers in their hair, and said nothing to me and nothing to each other, and I really thought my time had come. After they had eaten their breakfast they went on up the Platte River toward Fort Laramie. After we had traveled about three hundred miles we camped in the vicinity of a large Indian force under the control of Spotted Tail. I was with a group of men that had gathered when I felt a tug at my coat tail. I looked around quickly but saw no one, so I went on speaking to the man that I had been talking to. Pretty soon I felt another tug, and looking around saw an Indian, whom I recognized as the leader of the band that had eaten breakfast at our camp a few days before. The Indian told me that his name was Spotted Tail, and that he wanted me to come to his camp a few miles away. I told him I would go. Although the others in the party tried to dissuade me from the undertaking, I went. The chief treated me with great kindness and hospitality. He was a tall, athletic Indian, and his daughters were very pretty, having regular features and black hair. I returned to the train well pleased with my visit. Forty years after, while at the World's Fair, I met a young man who had some office at Fort Laramie, which post Spotted Tail often visited. He told me that Spotted Tail often inquired about me, said that he had never been so well treated by a white man in his life, and expressed a desire to have me come and see him. I was very sorry that I never went through the reservation where Spotted Tail lived to stop off and see him."

"The Indians have massacred all the white settlers on White River and are coming down on us here in Puyallup," was passed from house to house on that fateful October day of 1855. Mrs. Woolery and Mrs. Boatman were the only survivors present at the reunion who witnessed the scenes that followed. Some had wagons; some had none. Strive as best they could, they only got across the river the first day. Two canoes were lashed together and the wagons ferried across, after being first taken apart. The trip out the next day was made on foot, the women carrying the young children on their backs. Then came the volunteer company a week later to rescue the provisions, stock, clothing and other property that had been abandoned. This party consisted of the settlers of the valley, with a few others—nineteen in all. The author was one of the "others," not having yet settled in the valley. As we went in by the "lower" road the column of United States troops and volunteers abandoned the field and withdrew by the "upper" road, leaving our little band in utter ignorance of our danger for four days, when we crossed the trail of the retreating column, which we afterwards learned had halted at Montgomery's, at the edge of the prairie. Our women folks were disturbed at our long stay, and the troops were under orders to advance to our rescue, when lo! and behold! at nightfall on the sixth day we returned, loaded with property and provisions, in most cases being all the possessions of the owners who formed a part of the company, and there was great joy in camp. Not an Indian had been seen nor a shot fired, except to empty our guns to make sure that they would "go," as some of the men quaintly expressed it.

After looking back over the vista of years, none of the party could say that life had been a failure; there was the lady bordering close on eighty years; the gentleman eighty-four and past (Peter Smith), with the "kids" of the party past the sixty-eighth mark, yet one would scarcely ever meet a more cheerful and merry party than this of the reunion of the old settlers of 1855.

CHAPTER XXIII.

A Chapter on Names.

In the latter part of the seventeenth century that intrepid English traveler, Jonathan Carver, wrote these immortal words:

"From the intelligence I gained from the Naudowessie Indians, among whom I arrived on the 7th of December (1776), and whose language I perfectly acquired during a residence of five months, and also from the accounts I afterwards obtained from the Assinipoils, who speak the same tongue, being a revolted band of the Naudowessies; and from the Killistinoes, neighbours of the Assinipoils, who speak the Chipeway language and inhabit the heads of the River Bourbon; I say from these natives, together with my own observations, I have learned that the four most capital rivers on the continent of North America, viz.: the St. Lawrence, the Mississippi, the River Bourbon and the Oregon, or the River of the West (as I hinted in my introduction), have their sources in the same neighbourhood. The waters of the three former are within thirty miles of each other; the latter, however, is rather further west."

All students of history acknowledge this is the first mention of the word Oregon in English literature. The narrative quoted was inspired by his observations on the upper Mississippi, and particularly upon the event of reaching his farthest point, sixty miles above the Falls of St. Anthony, November 17th, 1776. This was the farthest up the Mississippi that the white man had ever penetrated, "So that we are obliged solely to the Indians for all the intelligence we are able to give relative to the more northern parts," and yet this man, seemingly with prophetic sight, discovered the great river of the West, attempted to name it, and coined a word for the purpose. While Carver missed his mark and did not succeed in affixing the new-born name to the great river he saw in his vision, yet the word became immortal through the mighty empire for which it afterwards stood. Carver made no explanation as to where the word Oregon came from, but wrote as though it was well known like the other rivers mentioned. Probably for all time the origin of this name will be a mystery.

We have a like curious phenomenon in the case of Winthrop first writing the word Tacoma, in September, 1853. None of the old settlers had heard that name, either through the Indians or otherwise, until after the publication of Winthrop's work ten years later, "The Canoe and The Saddle," when it became common knowledge and was locally applied in Olympia as early as 1866, said to have been suggested by Edward Giddings of that place.

However, as Winthrop distinctly claimed to have obtained the word from the Indians, the fact was accepted by the reading public, and the Indians soon took their cue from their white neighbors.

It is an interesting coincident that almost within a stone's throw of where Winthrop coined the name that we find it applied to the locality that has grown to be the great city of Tacoma.

On the 26th of October, 1868, John W. Ackerson located a mill site on Commencement Bay, within the present limits of the City of Tacoma, and applied the name to his mill. He said he had gotten it from Chief Spot of the Puyallup tribe, who claimed it was the Indian name for the mountain, Rainier.

The word or name Seattle was unknown when the founders of this city first began to canvass the question of selecting a site for the town, and some time elapsed before a name was coined out of the word Se-alth.

Se-alth, or Seattle, as he was afterwards known, was reported to be the chief of six tribes or bands, but at best his control was like most all the chiefs on the Sound, but shadowy.

Arthur Denny says that we (meaning himself, Boren and Bell), canvassed the question as to a name and agreed to call the place Seattle, after the old chief (Se-alth), but we have no definite information as to when the change in the old chief's name took place. Sealth was quite disturbed to have his name trifled with and appropriated by the whites, and was quite willing to levy a tribute by persuasion upon the good people of the embryo city.

I have another historic name to write about, Puyallup, that we know is of Indian origin—as old as the memory of the white man runs. But such a name! I consider it no honor to the man who named the town (now city) of Puyallup. I accept the odium attached to inflicting that name on suffering succeeding generations by first platting a few blocks of land into village lots and recording them under the name Puyallup. I have been ashamed of the act ever since. The first time I went East after the town was named and said to a friend in New York that our town was named Puyallup he seemed startled.

"Named WHAT?"

"Puyallup," I said, emphasizing the word.

"That's a jaw breaker," came the response. "How do you spell it?"

"P-u-y-a-l-l-u-p," I said.

"Let me see—how did you say you pronounced it?"

Pouting out my lips like a veritable Siwash, and emphasizing every letter and syllable so as to bring out the *Peuw* for Puy, and the strong emphasis on the *al,* and cracking my lips together to cut off the *lup,* I finally drilled my friend so he could pronounce the word, yet fell short of the elegance of the scientific pronunciation.

Then when I crossed the Atlantic and across the old London bridge to the Borough, and there encountered the factors of the hop trade on that historic ground, the haunts of Dickens in his day; and when we were bid to be seated to partake of the viands of an elegant dinner; and when I saw the troubled look of my friend, whose lot it was to introduce me to the assembled hop merchants, and knew what was weighing on his mind, my sympathy went out to him but remained helpless to aid him.

"I say—I say—let me introduce to you my American friend—my American friend from—my American friend from—from—from—"

And when, with an imploring look he visibly appealed to me for help, and finally blurted out:

"I say, Meeker, I cawn't remember that blarsted name—what is it?"

And when the explosion of mirth came with:

"All the same, he's a jolly good fellow—a jolly good fellow."

I say, when all this had happened, and much more besides, I could yet feel resigned to my fate.

Then when at Dawson I could hear the shrill whistle from the would-be wag, and hear:

"He's all the way from Puy-al-lup," I could yet remain in composure.

Then when, at night at the theaters, the jesters would say:

"Whar was it, stranger, you said you was from?"

"PUY-AL-LUP!"

"Oh, you did?" followed by roars of laughter all over the house. All this I could hear with seeming equanimity.

But when letters began to come addressed "Pewlupe," "Polly-pup," "Pull-all-up," "Pewl-a-loop," and finally

"Pay-all-up," then my cup of sorrow was full and I was ready to put on sackcloth and ashes.

The name for the town, however, came about in this way: In the early days we had a postoffice, Franklin. Sometimes it was on one side of the river, and then again on the other; sometimes way to one side of the settlement and then again to the other. It was not much trouble those days to move a postoffice. One could almost carry the whole outfit in one's coat pocket.

We were all tired of the name Franklin, for there were so many Franklins that our mail was continually being sent astray. We agreed there never would be but one Puyallup; and in that we were unquestionably right, for surely there will never be another.

Nevertheless, people would come and settle with us. Where the big stumps and trees stood and occupied the ground, we now have brick blocks and solid streets. Where the cabins stood, now quite pretentious residences have arisen. The old log-cabin school house has given way to three large houses, where now near eight hundred scholars are in attendance, instead of but eleven, as at first. And still the people came and built a hundred houses last year, each contributing their mite to perpetuating the name Puyallup. Puyallup has been my home for forty years, and it is but natural I should love the place, even if I cannot revere the name.

OLDEST BELL TOWER ON AMERICAN CONTINENT, TACOMA, WASH.
GIANT FIR, 500 YEARS OLD.

CHAPTER XXIV.

Pioneer Religious Experiences and Incidents.

If we were to confine the word religion to its strict construction as to meaning, we would cut off the pioneer actions under this heading to a great extent; but, if we will think of the definition as applied to morality, the duties of man to man, to character building—then the field is rich. Many of the pioneers, necessarily cut loose from church organizations, were not eager to enter again into their old affiliations, though their conduct showed a truly religious spirit. There were many who were outside the fold before they left their homes, and such, as a class, remained as they were; but many showed a sincere purpose to do right according to the light that was in them, and who shall say that if the spirit that prompted them was their duty to man, that such were not as truly religious as if the higher spiritual motives moved them?

We had, though, many earnest workers, whose zeal never abated, who felt it a duty to save souls, and who preached to others incessantly, in season and out of season, and whose work, be it said, exercised a good influence over the minds of the people.

One instance I have in mind—Father Weston, who came at irregular intervals to Puyallup, whose energy would make amends for his lack of eloquence, and whose example would add weight to his precepts. He was a good old man. Almost everyone would go to hear him, although it was in everybody's mouth that he could not preach. He would make up in noise and fervency what he lacked in logic and eloquence. Positively, one could

often hear him across a ten-acre lot when he would
preach in a grove, and would pound his improvised pul-
pit with as much vigor as he would his weld on his anvil
week days.

One time the old man came to the valley, made his
headquarters near where the town of Sumner now is,
induced other ministers to join him, and entered on a
crusade, a protracted union meeting, with the old-time
mourners' bench, amen corner and shouting members.
When the second Sunday came the crowd was so great
that the windows were taken out of the little school
house, and more than half the people sat or reclined on
the ground, or wagons drawn near by, to listen to the
noisy scene inside the house.

A peculiar couple, whom I knew well, had attended
from a distance, the husband, a frail, little old man, in-
tensely and fervently religious, while the wife, who was
a specimen of strong womanhood, had never been able
to see her way clear to join the church. Aunt Ann (she
is still living), either from excitement or to please the
husband, went to the mourners' bench and made some
profession that led Uncle John, the husband, to believe
the wife had at last got religion. Upon their return
home the good lady soon began wavering, despite the
urgent appeals from the husband, and finally blurted
out:

"Well, John, I don't believe there is such a place as
hell, anyhow."

This was too much for the husband, who, in a fit of
sheer desperation, said:

"Well, well, Ann, you wait and you'll see." And the
good lady, now past eighty, is waiting yet, but the good
little husband has long since gone to spy out the land.

I have known this lady now for fifty years, and although she has never made a profession of religion or
joined a church, yet there has been none more ready to
help a neighbor or to minister to the sick, or open the

door of genuine hospitality than this same uncouth, rough-spoken pioneer woman.

I recall one couple, man and wife, who came among us of the true and faithful, to preach and practice the Baptist Christian religion. I purposely add "Christian," for if ever in these later years two people embodied the true Christ-like spirit, Mr. and Mrs. Wickser did—lived their religion and made their professions manifest by their works.

Mrs. Wickser was a very tall lady of ordinary appearance as to features, while the husband was short and actually deformed. The disparity in their heights was so great that as they stood or walked side by side he could have gone beneath her outstretched arm. Added to this peculiar appearance, like a woman and a boy of ten years parading as man and wife, the features of the little man riveted one's attention. With a low forehead, flattened nose, and swarthy complexion, one could not determine whether he was white or part red and black, Chinaman or what not; as Dr. Weed said to me in a whisper when he first caught sight of his features: *"What,* is that the missing link?" In truth, the Doctor was so surprised that he was only half in jest, not at the time knowing the "creature," as he said, was the Baptist minister of the place.

But, as time went on, the strangeness of his features wore off, and the beauty of his character began to shine more and more, until there were none more respected and loved than this couple, by those who had come to know them.

A small factory had been established not far from the school house, where we had our Christmas tree. Some of the men from the factory took it into their heads to play what they called a joke on Mr. and Mrs. W. by placing on the tree a large bundle purporting to be a present, but which they innocently opened and found to contain a direct insult.

The little man, it could be seen, was deeply mortified, yet made no sign of resentment, although it soon became known who the parties were, but treated them with such forbearance and kindness that they became so ashamed of themselves as to inspire better conduct, and so that night the most substantial contribution of the season was quietly deposited at the good missionary's door, and ever after that all alike treated them with the greatest respect.

I have known this couple to walk through storm as well as sunshine, on roads or on trails, for miles around, visiting the pioneers as regularly as the week came, ministering to the wants of the sick, if perchance there were such, cheering the discouraged or lending a helping hand where needed, veritable Good Samaritans as they were, a credit to our race by the exhibition of the spirit within them.

Take the case of George Bush, the negro, who refused to sell his crop to speculators for cash, yet distributed it freely to the immigrants who had come later, without money and without price. Also Sidney Ford, another early rugged settler, although neither of them church members. Who will dare say theirs were not religious acts?

In response to a letter, the following characteristic reply from one of the McAuley sisters will be read with interest, as showing "the other sort" of pioneer religious experience, and following this, the brother's response about the "mining camp brand." She writes:

"And now as to your question in a former letter, in regard to religious experiences of pioneers. Tom had written me just before your letter came, asking if I had heard from friend Meeker and wife. I told him of your letter and asked him if he ever heard of such a thing as religious experience among pioneers. I enclose his answer, which is characteristic of him. The first church service I attended in California was in a saloon, and the congregation, comprising nearly all the inhabitants of the place, was attentive and

orderly. I think the religion of the pioneers was carried in
their hearts, and bore its fruit in honesty and charity rather
than in outward forms and ceremonies. I remember an instance on the plains. Your brother, O. P., had a deck of
cards in his vest pocket. Sister Margaret smiled and said:
'Your pocket betrays you.' 'Do you think it a betrayal?'
said he. 'If I thought it was wrong I would not use them.'
Here is Brother Tom's letter:

" 'Why, of course, I have seen as well as heard of pioneer
religious experiences. But I expect the California mining
camp brand differed some from the Washington brand for
agricultural use, because the mining camp was liable to lose
at short notice all its inhabitants on discovery of new dig-
gings.'

"So, of course, large church buildings for exclusive church
purposes were out of the question as impossible. And the
only public buildings available were the saloons and gam-
bling halls, whose doors, like the gates of perdition, were always open, day and night alike, to all, saint or sinner, who
chose to enter, and having entered, had his rights as well as
his duties well understood, and if need be, promptly enforced."

John McLeod used to almost invariably get gloriously
drunk whenever he came to Steilacoom, which was quite
often, and generally would take a gallon keg home with
him full of the vile stuff. And yet this man was a regular reader of his Bible, and, I am told by those who
knew his habits best, read his chapter as regularly as
he drank his gill of whisky, or perhaps more regularly,
as the keg would at times become dry, while his Bible
never failed him. I have his old, well-thumbed Gaelic
Bible, with its title page of 1828, which he brought with
him to this country in 1833, and used until his failing
sight compelled the use of another of coarser print.

I am loth to close this (to me) interesting chapter,
but my volume is full and overflowing and I am admonished not to pursue the subject further. A full volume
might be written and yet not exhaust this interesting
subject.

CHAPTER XXV.

Wild Animals.

I will write this chapter for the youngsters, and the elderly wise-heads who wear specs may turn over the leaves without reading it, if they choose.

Wild animals in early days were very much more plentiful than now, particularly deer and black bear. The black bear troubled us a good deal and would come near the houses and kill our pigs; but it did not take many years to thin them out. They were very cowardly and would run away from us in the thick brush, except when the young cubs were with them, and then we had to be more careful.

There was one animal, the cougar, we felt might be dangerous, but I never saw but one in the woods. Before I tell you about it I will relate an adventure one of my own little girls had with one of these creatures near by our own home in the Puyallup valley.

I have written elsewhere about our little log cabin school house, but have not told how our children got to it. From our house to the school house the trail led through very heavy timber and *very* heavy underbrush —so dense that most all the way one could not see, in the summer time when the leaves were on, as far as across the kitchen of the house.

One day little Carrie, now an elderly lady (I won't say how old), now living in Seattle, started to go to school, but soon came running back out of breath.

"Mamma! Mamma! I saw a great big cat sharpening his claws on a great big tree, just like pussy does," she said as soon as she could catch her breath. Sure enough, upon examination, there were the marks as high up on the tree as I could reach. It must have been a big one to reach up the tree that far. But the incident soon dropped out of mind and the children went to school on the trail just the same as if nothing had happened.

The way I happened to see the cougar was this: Lew. McMillan bought one hundred and sixty-one cattle and drove them from Oregon to what we then used to call Upper White River, but it was the present site of Auburn. He had to swim his cattle over all the rivers, and his horses, too, and then at the last day's drive brought them on the divide between Stuck River and the Sound. The cattle were all very tame when he took them into the White River valley, for they were tired and hungry. At that time White River valley was covered with brush and timber, except here and there a small prairie. The upper part of the valley was grown up with tall, coarse rushes that remained green all winter, and so he didn't have to feed his cattle, but they got nice and fat long before spring. We bought them and agreed to take twenty head at a time. By this time the cattle were nearly as wild as deer. So Lew. built a very strong corral on the bank of the river, near where Auburn is now, and then made a brush fence from one corner down river way, which made it a sort of a lane, with the fence on one side and the river on the other, and gradually widened out as he got further from the corral.

I used to go over from Steilacoom and stay all night so we could make a drive into the corral early, but this time I was belated and had to camp on the road, so that we did not get an early start for the next day's drive. The cattle seemed unruly that day, and when we let them out of the corral up river way, they scattered and we couldn't do anything with them. The upshot of the matter was that I had to go home without any cattle.

We had worked with the cattle so long that it was very late before I got started and had to go on foot. At that time the valley above Auburn near the Stuck River crossing was filled with a dense forest of monster fir and cedar trees, and a good deal of underbrush besides. That forest was so dense in places that it was difficult to see the road, even on a bright, sunshiny day, while on a cloudy day it seemed almost like night, though I could see well enough to keep on the crooked trail all right.

Well, just before I got to Stuck River crossing I came to a turn in the trail where it crossed the top of a big fir that had been turned up by the roots and had fallen nearly parallel with the trail. The big roots held the butt of the tree up from the ground, and I think the tree was four feet in diameter a hundred feet from the butt, and the whole body, from root to top, was eighty-four steps long, or about two hundred and fifty feet. I have seen longer trees than that, though, and bigger ones, but there were a great many like this one standing all around about me.

I didn't stop to step it then, but you may be sure I took some pretty long strides about that time. Just as I stepped over the fallen tree near the top I saw something move on the big body near the roots, and sure enough the thing was coming right toward me. In an instant I realized what it was. It was a tremendous, great big cougar. He was very pretty, but did not look very nice to me. I had just had a letter from a man living near the Chehalis telling me of three lank, lean cougars coming into his clearing where he was at work, and when he started to go to his cabin to get his gun the brutes started to follow him, and he only just escaped into his house, with barely time to slam the door shut. He wrote that his dogs had gotten them on the run by the time he was ready with his gun, and he finally killed all three of them. He found they were literally starving and had, he thought, recently robbed an Indian

grave, or rather an Indian canoe that hung in the trees
with their dead in it. That is the way the Indians used to
dispose of their dead, but I haven't time to tell about
that now. This man found bits of cloth, some hair, and
a piece of bone in the stomach of one of them, so he felt
sure he was right in his surmise, and I think he was, too.
I sent this man's letter to the paper, the Olympia *Transcript,* and it was printed at the time, but I have forgotten his name.

Well, I didn't know what to do. I had no gun with
me, and I knew perfectly well there was no use to run.
I knew, too, that I could not do as Mr. Stocking did,
grapple with it and kick it to death. This one confront-
ing me was a monstrous big one—at least it looked so to
me. I expect it looked bigger than it really was. Was
I scared, did you say? Did you ever have creepers run
up your back and right to the roots of your hair, and
nearly to the top of your head? Yes, I'll warrant you
have, though a good many fellows won't acknowledge it
and say it's only cowards that feel that way. Maybe;
but, anyway, I don't want to meet wild cougars in the
timber.

Mr. Stocking, whom I spoke about, lived about ten
miles from Olympia at Glasgow's place. He was walking on the prairie and had a stout young dog with him,
and came suddenly upon a cougar lying in a corner of
the fence. His dog tackled the brute at once, but was no
match for him, and would soon have been killed if Stocking had not interfered. Mr. Stocking gathered on to a
big club and struck the cougar one heavy blow over the
back, but the stick broke and the cougar left the dog and
attacked his master. And so it was a life and death
struggle. Mr. Stocking was a very powerful man. It
was said that he was double-jointed. He was full six
feet high and heavy in proportion. He was a typical
pioneer in health, strength and power of endurance. He
said he felt as though his time had come, but there was

one chance in a thousand and he was going to take that chance. As soon as the cougar let go of the dog to tackle Stocking, the cur sneaked off to let his master fight it out alone. He had had enough fight for one day. As the cougar raised on his hind legs Stocking luckily grasped him by the throat and began kicking him in the stomach. Stocking said he thought if he could get one good kick in the region of the heart he felt that he might settle him. I guess, boys, no football player ever kicked as hard as Stocking did that day. The difference was that he was literally kicking for dear life, while the player kicks only for fun. All this happened in less time than it takes me to tell it. Meanwhile the cougar was not idle, but was clawing away at Stocking's arms and shoulders, and once he hit him a clip on the nose. The dog finally returned to the strife and between the two they laid Mr. Cougar low and took off his skin the next day. Mr. Stocking took it to Olympia, where it was used for a base purpose. It was stuffed and put into a saloon and kept there a long time to attract people into the saloon.

Did my cougar hurt me, did you say? I hadn't any cougar and hadn't lost one, and if I had been hurt I wouldn't have been here to tell you this story. The fun of it was that the cougar hadn't yet seen me, but just as soon as he did he scampered off like the Old Harry himself was after him, and I strode off down the trail like old Belzebub was after me.

Now, youngsters, before you go to bed, just bear in mind there is no danger here now from wild animals, and there was not much then, for in all the time I have been here, now over fifty years, I have known of but two persons killed by them.

And now I will tell you one more true story and then quit for this time. Aunt Abbie Sumner one evening heard Gus Johnson hallooing at the top of his voice, a little way out from the house. Her father said Gus was just driving up the cows, but Aunt Abbie said she never knew him to make such a noise as that before, and went out within speaking distance and where she could see him at times pounding vigorously on a tree for awhile and then turn and strike out toward the brush and yell so loud she said she believed he could be heard for more than a mile away. She soon saw something moving in the brush. It was a bear. Gus had suddenly come upon a bear and her cubs and run one of the cubs up a tree. He pounded on the tree to keep it there, but had to turn at times to fight the bear away from him. As soon as he could find time to speak he told her to go to the house and bring the gun, which she did, and that woman went right up to the tree and handed Gus the gun while the bear was near by. Gus made a bad shot the first time and wounded the bear, but the next time killed her. But lo, and behold! he hadn't any more bullets and the cub was still up the tree. So away went Aunt Abbie two miles to a neighbor to get lead to mold some bullets. But by this time it was dark, and Gus stayed all night at the butt of the tree and kept a fire burning, and next morning killed the cub. So he got the hides of both of them. This occurred about three miles east of Bucoda, and both of the parties are living in sight of the spot where the adventure took place.

CHAPTER XXVI.

The Morning School.

And now I will write another chapter for the young-sters, the boys and girls, and the old folks may skip it if they wish; but I am going to relate true stories.

Soon after the Indian war we moved to our donation claim. We had but three neighbors, the nearest nearly two miles away, and two of them kept bachelor's hall and were of no account for schools. Of course, we could not see any of our neighbors' houses, and could reach but one by a road and the others by a trail. Under such conditions we could not have a public school. I can best tell about our morning school by relating an incident that happened a few months after it was started.

One day one of our farther-off neighbors, who lived over four miles away, came to visit us. Naturally, the children flocked around him to hear his stories in Scotch brogue, and began to ply questions, to which he soon responded by asking other questions, one of which was when they expected to go to school.

"Why, we have school now," responded a chorus of voices. "We have school every day."

"And, pray, who is your teacher, and where is your school house?" came the prompt inquiry.

"Father teaches us at home every morning before breakfast. He hears the lessons then, but mother helps us, too."

Peter Smith, the neighbor (and one of the group in the old settlers' meeting), never tires telling the story, and maybe has added a little as memory fails, for he is eighty-four years old now.*

"Your father told me awhile ago that you had your breakfast at six o'clock. What time do you get up?"

"Why, father sets the clock for half-past four, and that gives us an hour while mother gets breakfast, you know."

You boys and girls who read this chapter may have a feeling almost akin to pity for those poor pioneer children who had to get up so early, but you may as well dismiss such thoughts from your minds, for they were happy and cheerful and healthy, worked some during the day, besides studying their lessons, but they went to bed earlier than some boys and girls do these days.

It was not long until we moved to the Puyallup valley, where there were more neighbors—two families to the square mile, but not one of them in sight, because the timber and underbrush was so thick we could scarcely see two rods from the edge of our clearing. Now we could have a real school; but first I will tell about the school house.

Some of the neighbors took their axes to cut the logs, some their oxen to haul them, others their saws and frows to make the clapboards for the roof, while again others, more handy with tools, made the benches out of split logs, or, as we called them, puncheons. With a good many willing hands, the house soon received the finishing touches. The side walls were scarcely high enough for the door, and one was cut in the end and a door hung on wooden hinges that squeaked a good deal when the door was opened or shut; but the children did not mind that. The roof answered well for the ceiling overhead, and a log cut out on each side made two long,

*Smith has just died as this work is going through the press. He was one of our most respected pioneers, possessed of sterling qualities of manhood. Like Father Kincaid, he was without enemies.

narrow windows for light. The larger children sat with their faces to the walls, with long shelves in front of them, while the smaller tots sat on low benches near the middle of the room. When the weather would permit the teacher left the door open to admit more light, but had no need for more fresh air as the roof was quite open and the cracks between the logs let in plenty. You can see the face of one of the teachers on the opposite page who is now over eighty years of age.

Sometimes we had a lady teacher, and then her salary was smaller, as she boarded around. That meant some discomfort part of the time, where the surroundings were not pleasant.

Some of those scholars are dead, some have wandered to parts unknown, while those that are left are nearly all married and are grandfathers or grandmothers, but all living remember the old log school house with affection. This is a true picture, as I recollect, of the early school days in the Puyallup valley, when, as the unknown poet has said:

"And children did a half day's work
Before they went to school."

Not quite so hard as that, but very near it, as we were always up early and the children did a lot of work before and after school time.

When Carrie was afterwards sent to Portland to the high school she took her place in the class just the same as if she had been taught in a grand brick school house. "Where there is a will there is a way."

You must not conclude that we had no recreation and that we were a sorrowful set devoid of enjoyment, for there never was a happier lot of people than these same hard-working pioneers and their families. I will now

THE OLD SCHOOLMASTER

tell you something about their home life, their amusements as well as their labor.

Before the clearings were large we sometimes got pinched for both food and clothing, though I will not say we suffered much for either, though I know of some families at times who lived on potatoes "straight." Usually fish could be had in abundance, and considerable game—some bear and plenty of deer. The clothing gave us the most trouble, as but little money came to us for the small quantity of produce we had to spare. I remember one winter we were at our wits' end for shoes. We just could not get money to buy shoes enough to go around, but managed to get leather to make each member of the family one pair. We killed a pig to get bristles for the wax-ends, cut the pegs from a green alder log and seasoned them in the oven, and made the lasts out of the same timber. Those shoes were clumsy, to be sure, but they kept our feet dry and warm, and we felt thankful for the comforts vouchsafed to us and sorry for some neighbors' children, who had to go barefooted even in quite cold weather.

Music was our greatest pleasure and we never tired of it. "Uncle John," as everyone called him, the old teacher, never tired teaching the children music, and so it soon came about they could read their music as readily as they could their school books. No Christmas ever went by without a Christmas tree, in which the whole neighborhood joined, or a Fourth of July passed without a celebration. We made the presents for the tree if we could not buy them, and supplied the musicians, reader and orator for the celebration. Everybody had something to do and a voice in saying what should be done, and that very fact made all happy .

We had sixteen miles to go to our market town, Steilacoom, over the roughest kind of a road. Nobody had horse teams at the start, and so we had to go with ox teams. We could not make the trip out and back in one day, and did not have money to pay hotel bills, and so we would drive out part of the way and camp and the next morning drive into town very early, do our trading, and, if possible, reach home the same day. If not able to do this, we camped again on the road; but if the night was not too dark would reach home in the night. And oh! what an appetite we would have, and how cheery the fire would be, and how welcome the reception in the cabin home.

One of the "youngsters," fifty years old to-morrow, after reading "The Morning School," writes:

"Yes, father, your story of the morning school is just as it was. I can see in my minds's eye yet us children reciting and standing up in a row to spell, and Auntie and mother getting breakfast, and can remember the little bed room; of rising early and of reading 'Uncle Tom's Cabin' as a dessert to the work."

Near where the old log cabin school house stood our high school building now stands, large enough to accommodate four hundred pupils. In the district where we could count nineteen children of school age, with eleven in attendance, now we have one thousand and seven boys and girls of school age, three large school houses and seventeen teachers.

The trees and stumps are all gone and brick buildings and other good houses occupy much of the land, and as many people now live in that school district as lived both east and west of the mountains when the Territory was created in March, 1853. Instead of ox teams, and some at that with sleds, the people have buggies and carriages, or they can travel on any of the eighteen passenger trains that pass daily through Puyallup, or on street cars to Tacoma, and also on some of the twenty to twenty-four freight trains, some of which are a third of

a mile long. Such are some of the changes wrought in
fifty years since pioneer life began in the Puyallup valley.

Now, just try your hand on this song that follows,
one that our dear old teacher has sung so often for us, in
company with one of those scholars of the old log cabin,
Mrs. Frances Bean, now of Tacoma, who has kindly
supplied the words and music:

FIFTY YEARS AGO

How wondrous are the changes Since fifty years a - go, When

girls wore woolen dresses And boys wore pants of tow; And

shoes were made of cowhide And socks of homespun wool; And

children did a half-day's work Be - fore they went to school.

CHORUS.—Some fif - ty years a - go; Some fif - ty years a-

go; The men and the boys And the girls and the toys; The
work and the play, And the night and the day, The
world and its ways Are all turned around Since fif - ty years a - go.

VERSE 2D.

The girls took music lessons
  Upon the spinning wheel,
And practiced late and early
  On spindle swift and reel.
The boy would ride the horse to mill,
  A dozen miles or so,
And hurry off before 'twas day
  Some fifty years ago.   —CHO.

VERSE 3D.

The people rode to meeting
  In sleds instead of sleighs,
And wagons rode as easy
  As buggies nowadays;
And oxen answered well for teams,
  Though now they'd be too slow;
For people lived not half so fast
  Some fifty years ago   —CHO.

VERSE 4TH.

Ah! well do I remember
  That Wilson's patent stove,
That father bought and paid for
  In cloth our girls had wove;
And how the people wondered
  When we got the thing to go,
And said 'twould burst and kill us all,
  Some fifty years ago.   —CHO.